Wagon Trails

The Story of the Defrosting of Minnesota

■■■■■■■■■■

Helen Joos Cichy

Second edition
ISBN 0-9619663-4-3

MINN
977.6   OCLC   gift
Cic
6/29/06

Van Amber Publishers
P.O. Box 267
Menomonie WI 54751

Phone (715) 235 7702

To order, please see last page.

HELEN JOOS CICHY   1898-1988

Helen Joos Cichy was born in the village of Millerville, Minnesota on April 1, 1898 to Mary (Klein) and Fredrick Joos.

She attended the village parochial school, and as a young lady, sang in the Seven Dolors church choir. She was always active in religious activities, and for years assisted in duties pertaining to daily care of the church altar.

She was married to Anton Cichy in 1917, and gave her life to the country and farm she came to love. Here she found time in the long, cold winters after household duties for a family of six children to educate herself through home study course in the art of writing. She enjoyed writing short stories for the Historical Society of Alexandria after she retired. Her endeavors drew her to the University of Minnesota where she studied further and continued her research in history.

Her story, *The Defrosting of Minnesota,* begins with the frozen earth which was to become the State of Minnesota. It was published in 1977 when she was 79 years old. It is here reissued in her memory in the year 2001.

by her daughter,
Rita Cichy Van Amber

BIBLIOGRAPHY

This author hereby wishes to acknowledge and thank our state historical Reference Library for their use of all the illustrations and maps which they have graciously permitted the use of for my book.

Special thanks go to the Historical Society Reference Library at Topeka, Kansas for that most impressive photocopy of the *Woman and Child Gathering Chips.* They, too, have granted me permission of its use for this book.

The contents for the text has been gleaned from:

J.M. McClung, *Minnesota As It Is In 1870;*
William W. Folwell, *History of Minnesota;*
J.M. Patterson, Minnesota Historical
      Society - - *Minnesota's Postal*
      Service in the Early Days,
Mr. Ken Prentis, historian at Detroit Lakes,
      Minnesota;
Roseauu County historian - G. Arnold
      Graften, Wanaska, Minnesota

Helen Joos Cichy - 1898-1988

Historian and author, Helen Joos Cichy received distinguished recognition of her work in pioneer history in the publication of her book, *The Defrosting of Minnesota*, reissued under the title, *Wagon Trails*.

The Ramsey County Library System, headquartered in St. Paul Public Library, has placed the publication on its Permanent Historical Archives.

Cichy self-published her work in 1977. It depicts pioneer life as told and remembered by pioneers.

Cichy lived and wrote in the home in which she was born, located in Millerville, Minnesota. The house was built by her carpenter father, who was also affiliated in the construction of some of the oldest churches still used today in St. Paul and Minneapolis.

The village homestead was built at a time when the village was little more than a settlement with a mission church and a school.

Her story of her mother and father and the home she was born in follows elsewhere in this book.

TABLE OF CONTENTS

Chapter .... Page #

    I Under the Fourth Flag
       Minnesota Puts Down Her Roots 1
   II Territorial Government 10
  III Statehood--Its Benefits and Its Demands 18
  IV Northwestern Minnesota 27
   V Sources of the Mississippi 35
  VI Minnesota's Climate 39
 VII Ox Cart Trains and Their Drivers 50
VIII The Mail and Its Difficulties 60
  IX Minnesota's Wild Fruits 72
   X Transportation-Navigation-Railroads 79
  XI Education and Religion - Schools 96
 XII Life in the Pineries 106
XIII Life and the Staff of Life are the Chief
       Productions in Minnesota 115
XIV Bonanza Farming -
       Capitalists Turning Farmers 120
XV The Great Racial Clash of 1862 126
XVI The Native Neighbors 133
XVII Life on the Frontier 139
XVIII Women's Right on the Frontier --
       The Seven Demerling Sisters 148
XVIV A 1869 Check List
       of the Cost of Living 161
XX Minnesota's Valiant Women 164
XXI A Potpourri of Early Minnesota Bread
       Recipes, and Others 175
XXII Meat, Fowl and Fish on the Frontier 201
XXIII Beverages, Substitutes For 218
XXIV Our Nation's Calamities
       from 1770 through the 1870's 223
XXV Log House Construction 234

Mary Joos' Biography, by
Helen Joos Cichy 243

Picture Section

Order Blank ....(Last Page)

CHAPTER I

Under the Fourth Flag
Minnesota Puts Down Her Roots

From the time that the Mayflower, with its hungry, bedraggled humanity had landed on Cape Cod, until France had relinquished her sovereignty and title to Great Britain of that territory east of the Mississippi River in 1763, a century had elapsed.

Please take a slow moving vehicle with a

hard board seat and travel with me on the virgin sod trails to take a backward view to the beginning, when all Minnesota was still an impenetrable frozen wilderness.

The sixty-five days at sea had brought untold hardship to the one hundred and one passengers on board the Mayflower. For religious reasons they had left the Mother Country. During the long difficult days and nights on board the Mayflower they had formed a pact based upon doing the will of God only, and not that of man.

The first winter nearly half had died, but this had given further strength to the unity pact they had pledged themselves to. Through harsh physical labor these people laid the foundation for America's great agricultural abundance.

Throughout the entire next century Minnesota remained an unexplored wilderness. The only white men who entered were missionaries, explorers and fur traders. While explorations were attempted as early as 1362 by the Norsemen, no white man had survived here for long.

English law was technically paramount east of the Mississippi River, Spanish law west of the river. After the British had abandoned their posts in the Northwest Territory and France had ceded Louisiana, the Federal Government proceeded to explore and to occupy this vast possession in the Northwest.

It was President Thomas Jefferson who sent Zebulon Pike with a company of soldiers on an exploratory expedition and to achieve order among some of the British fur traders who refused to relinquish their rights to the United States after the Revolutionary War.

Through the aid of Zebulon Pike, the Dakota's (Sioux) sold the land at the junction of the Minnesota with the Mississippi Rivers. However, it was not until the year of 1819-20 that the Federal Government sent Colonel Leavenworth with a contingent of soldiers and officers to establish and erect a fort. The fort was named St. Anthony as it was near St. Anthony Falls. This name was later changed to Fort Snelling, which name it has retained to the present time.

The Fort soon became a "Hub" around

3

which a few settlers tried to found homes. For the most part these were the Selkirks who had wandered southward in search of better living conditions.

The first permanent settlement in Manitoba, called the Red River Colony, was founded by a Scotsman named Thomas Douglas, the Earl of Selkirk. Others from the East came in search for employment at the Fort, some were retired soldiers and surveyors who had brought their families. They soon cleared land to produce food for themselves and to sell at the Fort. The only business was at the Trading Post; this brought fur traders as well as Indians to buy produce.

During the years when Minnesota was but a No Man's Land, the colonists were struggling for freedom and relief from the tyranny of the Mother Country. Meanwhile, their activities encroached more and more upon the livelihood of the Indians, and during the anger, strife and warfare the tribes were weakened and thereby driven westward.

When the French missionary, Father

Alouez, worked to establish a Mission for the native Dakotas, he was not only met by the Hurons who had been driven out of New York but by their powerful enemies the Iroquois. Bitter battles were fought at LaPorte with bloody massacres which marked their course in early Minnesota history.

This unfortunate affair brought the Revolutionary War right to our doorsteps by way of these two tribes causing anxieties and bloodshed for many years to our native Indians. Even at that early date the North Star State was being drawn into the strife for freedom and liberty.

Among the survivors of the Mayflower was a Welshman, Edmund Rice, strong, hardworking and religious. His chief aim in life in the New World was for self-dependency for themselves and his children. They must have succeeded as history tells that this family was well represented in the fight for freedom and justice for the Red Man.

While Minnesota was still in its primeval

stage, in 1817 a son was born to Mr. & Mrs. Edmund Rice in Massachusetts whom they named Henry M. Rice. This lad was destined to play an important part in the development of our state. At a very tender age he was employed by the Federal Government as an assistant surveyor to investigate the future potential of the Sault St. Marie in Michigan. Having completed this task he received further employment as a post sutler in the United States Army.

Alone with all his worldly goods upon his back Henry M. Rice walked through Michigan, Wisconsin and into No Man's Land, which later became Minnesota. He traveled until he came to the Falls of St. Anthony. As he unstrapped his knapsack, he gazed in wonder at all this magnificence and said, "Here I will build my home." He meant every word, but being only twenty-two and penniless it was some years before this became a reality.

What a privilege it was for these early people to see Minnesota in all its primeval glory and magnificent splendor. A vast panorama of virgin timber -- towering pines, giant cottonwoods, hard white oaks, soft and hard maples, walnuts, light and the deepest purple blacks to mention but a few.

Rushing, tumbling waterfalls shimmering in the early sunlight. The thousands of crystal clear lakes, streams and rivers, their waters so pure it was called "Living Waters." To drill or dig within the earth for water was unknown and, as yet, unnecessary. Pure cool springs sprang up everywhere until the white man came with his ax and his saw.

What a triumph it must have been when after many years of explorations within a mass of ripening cranberries and marshy waters an embryonic beginning was located which led its waters into what was assured to be the Majestic Father of Waters.

Tender native grasses so thick and lush that cattle became lost while grazing. No boundaries, fences or man-made obstacles to hinder travel, the abundance of wildlife was still undisturbed by the hunters guns and traps.

Yet all this grandeur and natural beauty was

unappreciated by the early fur traders, voyageurs and the ox cart traders. The greed which influenced their vision was only of the magnitude of the "LOOT". They came to plunder the land and the natives of its great wealth in furs, hides and roots, and later its pines, and then return to their homelands as heroes.

The French fur traders deemed it their privilege to carry off this plunder in hides and furs. After the land was plundered of its natural resources, neither the traders nor the Indian objected to cede the land to the white man for settlements.

The dreams of the white families were of homes, schools, and the establishment of government under justice, liberty and equality. Settlers continued to come to live within the protected area of the Fort until the military found this too great a burden for their limited budget and space, so they were expelled.

This act by the military made it necessary to make land available for all these citizens as well as for those yet to come. Yes; for the thousands yet to come. It is about these Americans that this manuscript has been compiled and written.

CHAPTER II

Thirty years had elapsed since Fort St. Anthony was established and renamed Fort Snelling. Mendota, the first village in our state, had become an organized Trading Post by 1828. That land be made available for purchase by the settlers already here was now of utmost importance.

Credit is due to General H. H. Sibley for having secured a territorial form of government in 1849. Without any credentials he appeared before congress to represent the settlers in that part of the territory of Wisconsin (Minnesota east of the river) which had been excluded from the State of Wisconsin when it was admitted into the Union.

As a delegate he secured the passage of establishing the territory of Minnesota; that act reserved to the future state two sections in each township for school purposes. He also secured a reservation of two townships for a State University. Finally, the sale of lands could now go forward for homesteads.

Henry M. Rice was now no longer a young man, his dream of a homestead could now be fulfilled, and he was among the first to make his eighty acre purchase in where the city of St. Paul was soon after located. Rice County and Rice Street were named in his honor. His statue has been erected in Statuary Hall of the United States Capitol by the State of Minnesota in 1916.

To make it possible for Territorial Rights to be granted, the lands owned by the Winnebagoes needed to be ceded to the Federal Government. The Winnebagoes placed their confidence in Henry M. Rice by sending him as a delegate to represent their tribe in the sale of their lands to the

Federal Government.

The Winnebagoes were so pleased with the honest treaty Henry M. Rice had negotiated for them that as a Commissioner he assisted in securing accession by the government to all the Sioux and Chippewa lands, covering the greater part of Minnesota.

Throughout all these negotiations Henry M. Rice retained the confidence of the Indians, he was called by them 'Wab-bee-mah-no-min", meaning White Rice.

Governor Ramsey was appointed by President Taylor as first Territorial Governor. He, as well as General Sibley and Henry M. Rice made their homes in Mendota. On the day Governor Ramsey entered upon his executive duties as governor he paddled across the river in a birch bark canoe from the home of General H. H. Sibley.

The California gold rush in 1848 brought a new influx of settlers into Minnesota Territory, mostly from east New York State, Pennsylvania and the New England States. These were the settlers who laid the foundation to make school a state institution. The New England Town Organization was embedded into the Constitution.

St. Paul soon took the lead of furthering territorial interests into achieving Statehood. The first court session was held at St. Anthony and Mendota respectively. It is interesting to note that only one man on the jury panel wore boots, Minnesota was still in the moccasin stage.

The territory grew by leaps and bounds and could no longer be held back. Through the efforts of General H. H. Sibley, who was a Delegate in Congress, Statehood was achieved on May 11, 1858.

Shortly before this, Senator A. Douglas had secured for the settlers the priority rights to pre-emption of unsurveyed lands against purchase by speculators.

Schools and churches or houses of worship

were established long before territorial days. The early missionaries made attempts to instruct the native Indians as well as the traders who had come with evil intentions, but little impressions were left in spite of their untiring efforts and good deeds. Some cause of this failure was because the European missionaries could not comprehend, much less empathize with the Red Man's Heritage.

It remained for Americans, men and women of third and fourth generations of American blood flowing in their veins to bring civilization into Minnesota.

These courageous, hardy people knew how to win the respect of the Red Man and how to hold it. These were men and women in all stations of life, of different races and creeds but with one common goal, which was to live in peaceful co-existence with the Red Man's family as well as all the others who came from or were coming from all parts of the world by now.

The Trading Post at Medina was surely as good a school as any. Without any books, reading, arithmetic, geography and natural sciences were taught first hand and generously laced with morality, integrity and wisdom. Adversely, greed, avarice, intemperance as well as licentiousness was also learned there, and all through examples only.

With the arrival of families from the east, roads were hewn out of the wilderness so homesteads could be allocated to them, cabins were built and communities established. The Constitution was fresh in everyone's mind; they remembered every word and clause, every word had been written in strife and warfare.

The words of the First Amendment, "Congress shall make no law disrespecting an establishment or religion or prohibiting the free exercise thereof..." strengthened our early settlers into upholding the faith of their forefathers; they brought it with them and kept it nourished by continuous use.

Each home had its time for divine worship, children had regular periods of instructions and classes. In fact, their simple lives, fraught with dangers and hard work were one continuous religious act.   Not all parents could teach constructively, but always there was a willing neighbor who did.

The Sabbath was not always observed on a Sunday or Saturday, but on any day of the week which was most feasible for all to gather or when a Minister arrived. The most spacious cabin was the house of worship in winter or inclement weather. During summer months services were held beneath the boughs of an ancient tree. Services were conducted according to their beliefs, classes in reading, writing and arithmetic were given to adults as well as to children.

Theologians, doctors, lawyers, teachers and bankers came to put down roots in this impenetrable, frozen wilderness. St. Anthony, St. Paul and Stillwater had private schools before Minnesota had Territorial Rights. Schools were encouraged and provided for with all the means these early settlers had. The Instructor was always regarded as a highly respected gentleman. There was good reason as many times he was the only one who could read and write the English language. Women were seldom given the opportunity for higher education.

Public schools did not come into existence in Minnesota until the middle of the nineteenth century. There were no compulsory school laws, no free textbooks, not even a school building. One book often sufficed for all the pupils, McGuffy's Reader or a similar one, which was owned by the instructor who usually also served as their minister. Some had a slate but many used birch bark and a piece of charcoal from the fireplace to learn "writing and ciphering" which was considered all that was necessary.

After Minnesota was admitted into the Union, the provisions which had already been made during early territorial days were then finally put into effect. Not all at once, but step by tedious step.

It has taken a heap of living by many people of all sects, races and creeds to transform that impenetrable, frozen wilderness into what it is today.

CHAPTER III

Statehood -- Its Benefits And Its Demands

While Statehood brought many benefits to the citizens it also brought new demands, all of which required early attention from Governor Ramsey and his limited budget with which to secure knowledgeable help. Fortunately, in those days patriotism was high and every citizen considered it their patriotic duty to serve without pay wherever aid was needed.

All were, as yet, strangers in this untamed

land and vulnerable to the harsh climate. Those who came were, for the most part, strong minded, brawny specimens of humanity.

Land offices, post offices and mail routes were needed, surveying of all this vastness was of utmost urgency but proceeded so very slow. Counties and legislative districts were to be established, settlers to be assisted in securing their homes and, most of all, were transportation routes to be opened. The first routes through the wilderness were a veritable quagmire through all but the frozen months, and then the endless drifts of snow halted all travel. At the best, they were merely guides so the traveler could know he was going into the right direction and would eventually arrive at his destination. The ax as well as the musket were standard traveling equipment, without either no one would have ventured far.

At this point in our state's history, land promoters from amongst our citizens became actively engaged in land sales and promotions by every known method of those times. The yearbook printed in St. Paul was a favorite method, it being distributed amongst potential wealthy clients in other states. This not only brought settlers but gamblers with financial backing from the east and the south.

Not all but, fortunately for our young state, most of these comers used their new wealth in further development of the area in which they chose to locate.

Our early explorers brought the most favorable reports to the outside world. Jonathan Carver, an English traveler, wrote in 1781 in his diary, "Minnesota is a most delightful country abounding with all the necessities of life that grow spontaneously." He spoke of trees bending under their load of fruits, meadows covered with hops and many sorts of vegetables. The ground stored with useful roots and eminences a little distance from the river, from which one may have views that cannot be excelled or described.

Jean Nicolett, in his official report to the War Department in 1838-9, wrote; "Among the regions (adjoining the Coteau des Prairies) which appear to be the most favorable is the one watered by the Mankato or Blue Earth River, to which I have given the name of 'Undine Region.' This appears to be comprising the counties of Faribault, Blue Earth, Waseca, Watonwan and parts of Brown and Cottonwood Counties." He continues, "The great number of navigable tributaries of the Mankato spreading themselves out into the shape of a fan, the groups of lakes surrounded by well wooded hills, some wide spreading prairies with a fertile soil, others apparently less favored but open to improvement; the whole together bestow upon this region a most picturesque appearance. The country, embraced by the Minnesota River (lower St. Peter) and the Undine Region, exceeds any land on the Mississippi above the Wisconsin River.

"The forests of the valley on the right bank are connected by groves and small wooded streams of the adjoining prairies with the forest called Bois Franc (Big Woods)." Jean Nicollett gave the names of the varieties as soft maple, American and red elm, black walnut, the nettle tree, basswood and red and white ash.

Mr. Nicollett continues, "Though the Coteau, as now understood, is outside of the limits of Minnesota except where it cuts slightly the southwestern corner, it seems to embrace on its eastern slope nearly all the western counties of Minnesota south of the Minnesota River."

Nicollett continues, "I pitched my tents during three days about the groups of Shetek or Pelican Lakes that occupy a portion of the space forming the plateau of the Coteau des Prairies." He also wrote of lakes which would furnish eligible sites for villages such as were occupied by some of the Dakota tribes previous to wars waged against them by the Sac and Fox tribes on the Shetek, Benton and Spirit Lakes, which nearly exterminated the Dakotas. All the lakes mentioned are in Minnesota.

Jean Nicollett describes the Coteau des Prairies as a vast plain elevated 1,916 feet above sea level, this being at its northern extremity. On the western slope 60 miles west of Fort Pierre, he wrote, it may be 2,096 feet above sea level and 890 feet above Big Stone Lake. He described it as a beautiful country, magnificent beyond description.

Extending over the immense green turf that forms the basin of the Red River of the north are the forest capped summits of the Nautuers des Terres that surround the sources of the Mississippi, the granitic valley of the upper St. Peters, and the depression in which are Lake Traverse and Big Stone Lakes.

Among the interesting specimens of vegetation of this region were such roots and plants as hazel, red root, petersworth, alum root, tufted and American vedge, wood sorrel, Canadian cinquefoil, germander, southern lily, button snake root, Virginia strawberry, buffalo clover, and Indian turnip.

General J.W. Bishop, who traversed that part of the state in 1866 as U. S. Surveyor wrote, "Embracing the sources of the Redwood, Yellow Medicine, Cottonwood and Des Moine Rivers, in all our perambulations we have found the soil everywhere, except on the Coteau, of the best quality adapted to the raising of wheat or any other crop that can be grown in the settled parts of the state. The Coteau crosses the state boundary near the corner of township 110 and 111, ranges

46 and 47, and takes in the land west of Lake Benton."

He continues, "No finer country is found or needed anywhere; a grove of timber, a few acres enclosed for a garden, and for grain enough for home consumption is easily acquired. The stock may range over the prairie hardly needing any attention from May into November."

"The Redwood River is fringed with timber, some of the streams emptying into the Cottonwood have deep valleys filled with timber, and fine groves may be found near the lakes. The fine clear lakes have handsome beaches and are plentifully stocked with fish and fowl. The elk and the buffalo are often met as far east as Lake Shetak."

In 1849 Captain John Pope as topographical Engineer was commissioned by the U.S. Government to explore northwestern Minnesota, namely; Hennepin, Wright, Stearns, McLeod, Meeker, Kandiyohi, Lincoln, Todd, Douglas, Pope, Stevens, Otter Tail, Grant, Carver, Nicollett, Sibley, Chippewa, Traverse, Lac Que Parle and

Big Stone. This is his report, "The country which I have, in part, traversed embraces about one-third of the territory. It lies to the north and east of St. Peter's River (Minnesota) and to the north and west of the Mississippi, including within its borders about 60,000 square miles."

"I have traversed this area from north to south a distance of 500 miles. With the exception of a few swamps, I have not seen one acre of unproductive land. The examination of a portion of this land of the territory during this past summer has convinced me that nature has been even in her gifts of soil more generous than in her channels of communication which she has left to the enterprise and industry of man to complete what she has so well begun."

Captain John Pope had this to say about our navigable waters, "When it is known that the Mississippi is navigable for at least 400 miles of its course within this territory (north of St. Paul), the Red River of the north nearly an equal distance, the St. Peter (Minnesota) with an improvement of one point only for 120 miles, and the Jaques River through nearly three degrees of latitude, it becomes a matter of vast interest to the world to ascertain the capacities for agriculture and manufacture of a country so bountifully supplied by nature for outlets for her products. I know of no country where so many advantages are presented to the farmer and manufacturer."

Captain Pope referred to the Otter Tail Lake area as the garden spot of the northwest. He further comments, "The entire region of country in all directions for about fifty miles is among the most beautiful and fertile in the world. The fine scenery and open groves of oak timber, of winding streams connecting them, and beautifully rolling country on all sides renders this part of Minnesota the Garden Spot of the northwest."

"It's impossible in a report of this character to describe the feelings of admiration and astonishment with which we first beheld the charming country in the vacinity of these lakes."

CHAPTER IV

Northwestern Minnesota

Mr. Reuben B. Carlton, a native of New York, settled in Fond du Lac where he lived until his death. When he was with the Pacific Railroad exploring party he wrote the following report about Clay and Becker Counties and the valley of the Buffalo River, forty miles north of Otter Tail Lake.

"How exhilarating to gallop over a sea of flowers, a pathless expanse, plunging now and then into grass so high that horse and rider are almost submerged. The buffalo are gone; the ox and cow are coming to take their place. Sheep and horses will soon fatten on the rich pasturage of these hills. The highest grade of a railroad would not exceed thirty feet to the mile in crossing them.

"Here we have granite and limestone boulders and, in some places, beds of gravel brought, so the geologists inform us, from the far north and deposited here when the primeval ocean currents set southward over this then-submerged region. They are in the right place for the railroad, the stone will be needed for abutments to bridges and the gravel will be wanted for ballast.

"On our second day's march we came to a section of country that might, with propriety, be called the Park Region of Minnesota. It lies amid the highlands of the divide; think of undulating country, rounded hills and green slopes with countless lakes, calm pure waters amid the hills skirted by forests, fringed with rushes and waves rippling on the graveled beaches.

"Wild geese, ducks, loons, pelicans and

innumerable water fowl building their nests amid the reeds and rushes. This is their haunt; we see their tracks along the sandy beaches and we see them in flight. I do not forget that I'm seeing Minnesota at its best season, that it is mid-summer and that the winters here are long and severe. But our party are unanimous in their praises of this Park Region of Minnesota. The land is unsurveyed, the nearest pioneer is forty miles away, but land so inviting cannot long remain unsettled."

Captain John Pope wrote of the country between Sauk Rapids and White Bear Lake. "The entire section of country between the Mississippi and White Bear Lake and Lightening Lake is located in Pope County seventy-five miles west of Sauk Rapids. The Surface is gently undulating, the soil exceedingly fertile and the timber most abundant."

Colonel Abert in his official report in 1854 as Topographical Engineer describes the "Big Woods." "The four thousand square miles of this district is probably the finest tract of land in the northwest. The largest body of water between the

Mississippi and Missouri Rivers, with every variety of deciduous timber, beautiful lakes abounding in fish of most delicious flavor.

"This covers about one-sixth of the area, another sixth is covered with wet meadows with very high grass affording pasturage and hay. The balance is gently undulating and densely timbered. The soil is of inexhaustible fertility and offering the best locations for farms of any country we saw along the route."

Of the Red River Valley, Captain John Pope wrote, "The Valley of the Red River of the north is about 300 miles in length from north to south and one and fifty miles in breadth from east to west, is bounded on the west by the dividing ridge of the Coteau des Prairies and on the east by a line from the head of Red River through to the most eastern point of Red Lake -- an Empire in itself.

"The prairie country between the several crossings of the Red and Rush Rivers is high, level and astonishingly fertile. The Sheyenne River is navigable for barges one hundred and fifty miles. As a grazing country it is as remarkably fine as may easily be understood from the fact that the expedition of the past summer made a march of nearly a thousand miles with heavy loaded wagons over a country without roads and heavy from continued rains. The horses subsisted during the entire period on prairie grasses.

"There is a fine body of elegant pine timber in the northern part of Otter Tail County, enough to supply the Red River Valley for a long time, if economically used. The Red River is navigable nearly all summer for good-sized boats to Goose River Rapids north of Georgetown. Small boats can run two months of every season to Abercrombie or Breakenridge. Some snags need clearing from Grahams point to the Rapids making navigation troublesome but not dangerous. Flat boats can navigate as far as Lapham, three miles from Dayton. The Red River Lake is also navigable with flat boats."

Northern Minnesota was described by geologists and government officials as Red Lake, St. Louis, Itasca, Cass and Wadena counties as well as Beltrami and the east half of Pembina. They described this vast area as generally unsuitable for agricultural purposes but had immense fields of wild rice, abounds in valuable minerals, forests of pine and hardwoods. An exception was the estimated three thousand square miles on the north shore of Lake Superior and the two thousand square miles scattered throughout the pineries. Belts of excellent land were reported around most of the lakes. The east part of Pembina between Lake of the Woods and Red Lake was considered an impassible swamp in the days when the State was first surveyed.

It was named the Highland or Mountain District of the state, its summit being 1,680 feet above sea level, being the dividing ridge between the waters flowing south to the Gulf of Mexico and those flowing north to Hudson Bay. The hills north of Lake Superior were estimated to rise 1,200 to 1,300 feet above sea level.

This included an area of sixteen thousand four hundred square miles west of St. Louis and Carlton Counties, including the east one-half of Pembina. Down the southern slope of the dividing ridge the land stretched away in an easy undulating, level, sandy plain. The northern slope toward Red Lake was found to be less and the surface more broken.

Voyageurs found, "The canoe route down the Big Fork River, obstructed at one point by falls of fifteen feet, descend and in its whole course the current is more rapid than of the upper Mississippi. Timber grows over the entire district on that portion drained by the Mississippi.

"Roads -- From Crow Wing Village following the north bank of the Crow Wing River by the Olga Agency to the crossing, thirty-three miles, then to Otter Tail Lake, mail weekly. From Crow Wing Village, by Gull Lake and Pine River to the New Agency, on the south shore of Leech Lake, seventy miles, mail weekly. From the north shore of Leech Lake, by the west side of Cass, crossing the dividing ridge near Turtle Lake to the south shore of Red Lake, seventy miles."

A Geologist's notebook stated this report: "The whole of Cass Lake formerly covered by water. The area is fully equal in size to the state of Connecticut and is a plateau which at a period comparatively recent has been denuded of water probably by a sudden rupture at Pokegama Falls. A dam at Pokegama Falls twenty feet high may flood the entire area again, therefore this area cannot be settled. The entire district, including the southern slope, is undergoing a process of drainage so rapidly that a large addition to the tillable land of the state may be calculated upon at no distant future."

CHAPTER V

Sources Of The Mississippi

After Jean Nicollett's exploration of the creek which empties into Lake Itasca, he reported, "Its headwaters unite at a small distance from the hills whence they originate and form a small lake from which the Mississippi flows with a breadth of a foot and a half and a depth of one foot. It passes through two small lakes and gathers other tributaries until it finally empties into Lake Itasca fifteen to twenty feet wide and two to three feet deep, issuing from the lake sixteen feet wide and fourteen inches deep, beautifully transparent with a swift current; after an hour's descent the breadth of the stream enlarges to twenty-five feet and its depth at three feet."

The Summit Level of the Mississippi
at its Sources

Jean Nicollett continues, "So far at Pemidji Lake the Mississippi has received the contributions of ten rivers. Its wide and flattened bed completely covered by water presents a lake from forty to fifty miles square. Clogged up with aquatic plants with spaces of clear water looking like channels but among which it is difficult to discover the true source. For at certain seasons of the year it's nothing more than a marshy prairie or an interminable labyrinth of streams, rice lakes, meadows, bogs and cranberry swamps."

Lake Superior District
Of Northern Minnesota

As taken from Jean Nicollett's report, "Relatively, the high ranges and chains of hills which begin in Canada and cross into Minnesota north of Lake Superior may be termed mountains, although they only rise to a height of twelve hundred to thirteen hundred feet above the lake at the highest point and less than two thousand feet above the water. This district embracing Lake and St. Louis Counties north of Lake Superior is the mineral district where iron, copper and slate quarries are the most valuable resources.

"The valleys between these mountain ridges are often from five to six hundred feet below the summits and vary in width from one to two miles to narrow gorges not more than two or three hundred yards across.

"In the trap region rugged mountain scenery prevails. In the shistose and granitic belt, occasional knolls or low ridges with intervening lakes or swamps make up the scene. In the drift region lines of conical hills and irregular depressions constitute the main features of the country. All the hills, valleys and ridges are densely timbered with white cedar, birch, spruce, fir, pine, aspen, maple, ash and basswood.

"The agricultural soil of the district is well

adapted to the production of wheat, oats, potatoes and garden vegetables."

CHAPTER VI

Minnesota's Climate

Theory of the climate in Minnesota as taken from the Meteorological Journal kept in Fort Snelling in the years of 1847-8-9. January had sixteen days below zero temperature between eleven to twenty-two degrees below in 1847. January 1848 had five days below ranging from two degrees to twenty-four below zero. January 1849 had fourteen days below ranging from two to twenty-five below zero.

The men at the fort consoled themselves

with the knowledge that it was cold in other states, also. They received this information through telegraphic dispatches being sent or exchanged between the different military bases in the northwest.

Dr. Owen's official in 1851 reads, "Our experience has taught us to prefer forty degrees below to ten below with a gale in the face. Since it is usually very calm when the thermometer is so low it is not felt as when the mercury is higher with a stiff breeze. We do not mean that we have no wind in the winter, but merely that it is rarely windy during the cold terms. What wind we have is during the moderate almost entirely.

"From the Army register kept at Fort Snelling, twelve year observations show that the yearly average of south or southerly winds were 172 days or nearly half the year. We rarely have rain in winter. Rain has not fallen in winter but once in many years. Our winters are cold, bright and exhilarating with cold snaps lasting three to four days with the mercury falling from thirty to forty degrees below zero, rising higher as the sun rises. These extremes are rare. Many enjoy them for their tonic effect, their stimulating powers being remarkable.

"The air at such times being as calm as a May morning. This rarely causes suffering or interruption to outdoor business or amusements. In fact, winter is the gayest of our seasons, skating parties on the rivers and lakes bring out the young in spirit of all ages --whose sports are prolonged to ten o'clock at night.

"Race tracks on the ice bring out the fast horses, the hillsides are thronged with young Americans coasting with sled or cutter. The streets ring with a continuous jingle of sleigh bells and concerts, balls, masquerades, fairs and festivals occupy the long evenings. The winter runs the rounds of its brilliant nights with far less suffering and far more exhilaration than if these were warmed with the July sun.

"Spring plowing usually begins in April or earlier; wheat has been sown in March for several years. The springs are cool, lakes and rivers open between the twentieth of March and April first. The weather begins to warm up by May 15-20th;

sooner than this is unreliable. The main temperature of the spring at Fort Snelling is 45 degrees. These figures are from observations for thirty to thirty-five years observations at the different military posts.

"Summers -- while the weather gets quite warm there is nearly always a cooling breeze, relieving one of what would elsewhere be the depressing and debilitating effect of the summer's heat. Nights are nearly always cool and refreshing, cooling showers with splendid electric displays are frequent and nearly always occur at night. Main temperature seventy to seventy-six degrees.

"Autumn is simply a continuation of summer, mellowed with the subdued heat and chastened with the milder sunshine of Indian Summer, commencing in early October and continuing until the end of November makes our autumns the golden season and to all the most delightful.

"Frost seldom occurs earlier than the last of September."

State Geologist Clark wrote in his report the following, "The degree of the habitual transparency of the air, the serenity of the sky have an important influence, not only on the organic development of plants and the ripening of fruits, but also on the feelings and entire mental disposition of man."

Minnesota's First Settlers

All of Minnesota was Indian Territory until the time of Ratification of the Treaties in 1837. The military, under the command of Zebulon K. Pike, had only access to the limited area where Fort Snelling was located, and only for the benefit of the Indians.

No unauthorized person could legally enter, but the Selkirks and the Voyageurs came south as far as Fort Snelling as refugees and remained there as squatters. The Selkirks were an industrious people having come to Canada from the Isles of Scotland, Wales and Ireland; later ones were Swiss. They knew how to derive their living by tilling the soil and feeding cattle and sheep. They were a thrifty clan and in their crude way even religious and peaceful.

The Selkirks were driven out of Canada under most tragic circumstances. Many were murdered, many died of disease and privation, until their colony established by Lord Selkirk was totally destroyed. While some were driven even farther north, a few wandered south into Pembina to safety amongst the savage Dakotas.

Thereafter Lord Selkirk sailed to Europe returning with other colonists hoping to re-establish the colony. The Swiss found conditions at the colony most unacceptable, so they too began to wander into Pembina until the spring of 1826 when the Red River floods inundated the entire area bringing further suffering and disease. On June 24, 1826 approximately 243 of these people left Pembina in a group, most of these came as refugees to Fort Snelling. They were permitted to remain as squatters. As time went on they cleared land, built log homes, broke the virgin soil and planted gardens which they found ready sales for at the fort.

Their numbers increased not only in births, but each season brought additional "refugees" from the north. This went on until 1837. During the period of 1823-37 there was hardly a single year in which some more came as "squatters". It had been estimated that at least half of these remained in Minnesota while the others wandered farther to the south into French speaking communities.

When the "squatters" learned of the Ratification, they became concerned about losing all their acquired property again, whereupon they composed a letter of petition to the President at the White House asking to be compensated for the improvements they had made in Minnesota. They never received a reply to their petition. Instead Major Joseph Plympton arrived to act as Commanding Officer of the Fort in August, 1837. He did this in no uncertain ways. Immediately he set about to investigate the "squatters" and found that an unusual amount of timber had been cut and used as fuel on the Reserved Land. This in itself was an alarming situation. Should this continue, he wrote in his report, the Fort will soon run short of timber for its own use. The report he issued served to spread alarm among the "squatters" causing some to leave, but most remained.

It was more than two years later that they were forced to vacate. The population had now increased considerably, and having paid no attention to the warnings to leave which had been given them, on May 6, 1839 a garrison of soldiers removed them bodily amidst much fighting, wrecking of furniture and property, and killing of livestock. Their cabins were burned so they could not return. Truly unfortunate people, they were homeless again.

Some left the area and even the state, but the majority staked claims on land outside of the Fort's holdings. Nearly two decades had elapsed since the Fort was established and after all the non-military population was removed it began to function in a manner suitable to its name.

The Red River people were again refugees, but this time they staked claims on land which had been ceded by the government; however the Indians had not been paid, so it was still illegal.

The Indians complained but were solaced by the fact that Voyageurs were also among the newcomers who were now peddling whiskey while masquerading as traders.

One such character was Pierre Parrant, a Canadian Voyageur, who was the first to stake his claim approximately on the location where the Capital Building now stands. In June, 1838 he built a crude shanty in a secluded spot, all being heavily timbered in those early days. Here he soon set up his whiskey shop. Not for long, as Major Joseph Plympton soon tracked him down and banished him of his claim for illegally selling whiskey to the Indians and his soldiers at the Fort. The claim was later sold to Benjamin Gervais, a decent member of the Red River people.

The new settlers having filed their claims set about building cabins or even shanties in a haphazard manner on hillsides. The settlement remained nameless until Father Galtier, a French missionary priest from Mendota, arrived to gather them together again. He found 185 Catholics who were happy to have him come and two new landowners gave him land on which they erected a crude log Chapel.

This Chapel was blessed and dedicated to St. Paul, the Apostle of Nations, on the first day of November, 1841. As there was no historic reason to challenge or change the name, the settlement was soon called St. Paul's Landing and later as St. Paul, the Capitol of our State.

However, it was not until the summer of 1848 that the government was finally able to offer the sales to any of this land. The sales were then completed at the new land office at St. Croix Falls.

Now that they felt secure in their crude new surroundings, they lost no time to establish a school, a better church, a hotel and even a bank. Undoubtedly these were the first white settlers, but it took much longer until the rural areas could receive honest-to-goodness settlers who broke the virgin soil, planted it to produce crops to sustain themselves as well as these small communities.

With the exception of a small amount of

produce from gardens the entire subsistence for the white population was brought in by steam boats. Even forage for animals was imported into the state. It was yet to be proven that this impenetrable wilderness could be tamed to produce crops.

CHAPTER VII

The Ox Cart Trains and Their Drivers

The earliest recorded authentic settlement in the northern part of Minnesota Territory was the Trading Post established by a French trader and trapper by the name of Baptiste Cadotte. This was as early as 1798 and was located at the confluence of Clearwater and Red Lake Rivers, near Red Lake Falls.

In 1800 Alexander Henry was placed in charge of the Northwest Fur Company's operations on the Red River. In that year he established his Trading Post at Pembina, hoping to encourage friendship with the Red Man and develope trade with the Indian trappers. Alexander Henry remained in charge of the Northwest Fur Company until 1808. During this period he established trading posts along the route, one was in Grand Forks, North Dakota and another perhaps in Roseau. By this time the Cadotte Post had been long abandoned.

In 1840 Joe Rolette, a stalwart man of mixed blood -- more Indian than French, came to Pembina to take charge of the Post there. It was here that he met Norman Kittson and together these two men, both trappers and traders, established the Red River Trail and later the Ox Cart Train.

In 1857 Joe Rollete and Norman Kittson platted a townsite where the trail crossed the Red River, naming it Douglas. Enthralled, they predicted a great and beautiful city would some day grow out of this townsite, but it fell into disuse and eventual decay as had so many of the early trading posts. Today it is doubtful if there ever was more than this meager log building at the site.

When the legislature passed the act establishing Polk County, the county seat was named. Douglas.

However, the Ox Cart Train these two men established was the first form of transportation in Minnesota, and the only such conveyance ever to be established in any part of the world.

The following has been taken out of Mr. Ken Prentice's "Horse and Buggy Days of Detroit Lakes", 1970. My thanks goes to him for granting me permission to use it here. Ken Prentice is Detroit Lakes' historian and long time reporter.

"Burial sites and artifacts found in the area give vague hints as to who the people were who lived here before the advent of the white man. Camp sites and signs of villages, especially along the east side of the north shore of Detroit Lakes, indicates the Sioux and the Chippewas fought to keep the area for their own playgrounds.

"When St. Paul merged as a leading center, French fur traders at Fort Garry (now Winnepeg) and Pembina used ox carts to carry their winter's supply of furs to St. Paul to sell and to bring back to the distant settlements. For about thirty years, from 1830-1867, this trade flourished. It was a million-dollar a year business. It also depleted this vast area of buffalo, beaver, otter, mink, fisher, martin, muskrat and fox.

"In time there came to be three main Red River Ox Cart Trails. The first one came down the western side of the Red River to Big Stone Lake, then followed the Minnesota River to St. Paul. The second one came down the eastern side of the Minnesota and then down to St. Paul. The third, called the Woods Trail, was the one that came through the Detroit Lakes Area. It was the shortest and most direct route, but it also posed the most problems because of the many lakes and streams. It was used when the Sioux Indians were on the warpath because it led through the Chippewa country; the Chippewa's were always friendly with the traders and ox cart men. The ox cart was the most unusual means of transportation ever devised. Made entirely of wood, it evolved into a vehicle capable of carrying eight hundred pounds of furs and pelts, mounted on spoke wheels six feet in diameter. The higher the wheels, the better it was for crossing marshes and muddy streams.

"Each wheel produced its own peculiar tone. The squeak of the wheel revolving on an axle that was never greased could be heard for several miles on a still day. A train of carts which sometimes numbered five hundred or more moving single file over the trail would broadcast a weird symphony of creaking music. It was learned by experience that ox carts could best be operated in 'trains' with a responsible leader in charge. The train was divided into brigades of twelve carts under the command of three drivers. The owners and drivers were half-breed French and Chippewa men called 'metis'. They hauled furs from Pembina and Winnepeg (Fort Garry) and took back such supplies as were needed, including mail, food and whiskey. The oxen plodded along at about fifteen miles per day; the four hundred mile trip took from thirty to forty days.

"They always brought their families with them; a six hundred cart train would include twelve hundred women and children. The stopover at St. Paul was a happy experience and reunion. In rainy weather the wheels sank into lowlands, marshes and mosquitoes tortured man and beasts. Floods, extreme heat or hostile Sioux might plague them, but the Metis seemed to enjoy this kind of life. Each day they got under way at dawn and the long train crept along at this slow pace until mid-afternoon when they stopped to make camp.

"The carts lined up into a rough circle, wheel to wheel, to form an enclosure. Inside this ring tepees whisked up, while some draped buffalo hides over their carts and slept underneath. The animals were allowed to graze freely until dark, when they were herded inside the enclosure. Throughout the night thirty to forty men stood guard. The rest of the people gathered around the campfire and danced and sang far into the early hours."

The trails which the ox cart trains traveled may have been earlier Indian trails. It is known that the Sioux tribes used these routes in their migrations throughout their vast territory. As civilization advanced, villages and cities sprang up along these routes that began as trading posts for the fur trades. When the stage coaches came into use, these same routes were used where possible. As the railroads were built they too used the same trails and routes as guides.

The Voyageur of the 19th Century

Guides were necessary as soon as the earliest explorers, traders, geologists and missionaries came into what we now refer to as the boundary waters between the nations. Seemingly, the Voyageur was born soon after the first Europeans came to the western continent to trap, trade and establish this trade with the Red Man who was still in the stone age.

These sons of Europeans having Indian mothers grew into stalwart men, dark of skin, hair often curly, and eyes not always dark. They came naturally endowed with the gift of their mothers tongue as well as that of their fathers. Through their mothers they learned the ways of the wilderness, later they were taken to Europe to learn and adapt themselves to civilization and Christianity.

Therefore, these men who had earned the right to call themselves "Voyageurs" were well trained, competent guides for the many who came as traders, trappers, prospectors, promoters or missionaries; all of whom came to live off the land and waters so bountifully endowed by our Creator with all that the white man coveted.

Rivers, lakes and streams were the highways for the Voyageurs. His boots were styled according to the moccasins his mother taught him to make. During hot, summer days he wore a blue jacket and wide brimmed hat of European style. The Voyageur's felt hat often sported a gayly colored plume, but only if he had earned that coveted award through the ability and experience of having become an expert oarsman of a twelve to sixteen man canoe, or excellence in oarsmanship.

The Voyageurs were in the employ of the fur companies. The Northwest Fur Company had its headquarters in Montreal and trading posts strung along the border waters of upper Minnesota. All the Voyageurs that plied these waters were employed by this company. A fort was constructed at Charlotte which served as a great depot. Much of the success of the Northwest Fur Company was due to their Voyageurs who traveled continually by canoe from post to post meeting trappers and traders as far west as the Dakotas with cargos of munitions, clothing, food, medicines, and often times fire water "to clear their throats." They traded with the Indians as well as with the white man, always returning with cargos of hides and pelts.

After the waters were frozen, they took to dog sleds, their dogs being reared and trained by the Voyageurs themselves. The Voyageurs were equally competent in constructing their crude log buildings; all was done with the use of a common ax -- no broad ax was known about at that early stage of our civilization in Minnesota. The Voyageurs constructed their own canoes according to the work they were to undertake.

As might be expected, there was often great jealousy between them and the men working for the Hudson Bay Company, as well as the Indians. Many a bloody battle was fought between these parties for possession of the best hunting grounds or the best streams and rivers. Due to the extensive hunting and trapping of all these men, the fur bearing animals dwindled in numbers to the extent that the trading posts were abandoned one by one, until finally the fur companies began to deteriorate until they ceased to exist by the end of the war in 1812.

Thereafter, the Voyageur worked for private parties, traders, trappers, and the missionaries, until the lumberjack with his ax and saw came upon the scene. What the Voyageur had preserved, the lumber men came to destroy. This led to bitterness, anger and many a battle, but the lumber men with their hard-soled heavy leather boots came to stay.

As the land became stripped of its valuable timber and put up for sale or free to homesteaders, many of the Canadian families, formerly Voyageurs, soon came to take advantage of this opportunity. They soon joined the many foreigners to help build Minnesota into what it is today.

CHAPTER VIII

The Mail And Its Difficulties

Our mail has always played an important part in the history of Minnesota. Even in this day of almost instant communication to all parts of the world, we still look forward eagerly for the day's mail.

The United States mail is today's biggest bargain. In the early days rates were based upon distance and envelopes were not yet in use. The written sheet was folded and sealed with wax.

Postage per sheet was six cents for thirty miles, ten cents for eighty miles, twelve and one-half cents for one hundred and fifty miles, while twenty-five cents paid for any distance beyond four hundred miles.

One shudders to think what conditions must have been like when in August 1819 the members of the U. S. Fifth Infantry Division received notice from the government in Washington to travel into the impenetrable wilderness of "No Man's Land" (Minnesota) to establish a fort there. Hundreds of miles of wilderness separated these men from family, friends and home. Their only connection with the civilized world was through the mail; the mail which did not arrive daily, or weekly, nor even monthly.

In summer mail would arrive two or three times during the season, having been delivered by canoes or keel boats from Prairie du Chien, a distance of over two hundred miles.

Keel boats were slow, heavy moving freight craft bringing supplies and the mail from

St. Louis to Prairie du Chien. In winter this trip was one wrought with hardships and dangers. It was made by runners, men hired to make the entire four hundred mile round trip on foot, over ice, a dog or pony hitched to a low sled was used to carry the mail. The trip took three weeks.

The runners were usually soldiers hired by the Indian Agent and were paid for doing the job. Simultaneously they carried army dispatches by orders of their commanding officer.

Lawrence Taliofero (pronounced Tolaver) was the agent at this time. He was a most dedicated and conscientious man, always being at work keeping the lines of communication open. The following has been taken from his writings. "Lieutenant Russell and Baxley have returned this afternoon from their trip to Prairie du Chien (sic). A mail was received by these gentlemen. The first for five months. On February 2 Dr. Harvey arrived from Prairie du Chien--brought a small mail. Received a letter from Virginia dated seven months since."

The first post office in the wilderness of

early Minnesota was established at Fort Snelling on August 25, 1827. The postmaster was John Garland.

After the freeze-up the following winter, Lawrence Taliofero hired an Indian runner named Okarpe to make the trip on foot to Prairie du Chien for the mail. Okarpe left Fort Snelling on December 3rd and returned December 24th with many letters and newspapers. This Christmas gift was gratefully received bringing much joy to all.

As pay, Okarpe received ten pounds of tobacco, ten pounds of lead, four pounds of gun powder, as well as other smaller items, plus an order on the American Fur Company for merchandise worth $9.25. The Commander made the Indian a gift of three and one-half gallons of whiskey. This information was found in Taliofero's Journals at the Minnesota Historical Society.

In addition to the hired runners, volunteers coming from Prairie du Chien would bring the mail as a gesture of kindness. These men were usually the fur traders traveling the route. Such haphazard mail deliveries continued until 1832.

Then Minnesota's Outpost had regular mail deliveries provided through U.S. Colonel Zachary Taylor, later President of the United States. He was, at that time, in command at Fort Crawford. During his tour of duty at Fort Snelling four years earlier he wrote, "We are here entirely out of the world and very seldom hear from the civilized parts of our country, as we have no regular mails." As a result of this, he detailed a soldier named James Halpin to carry the mail between Fort Crawford and Fort Snelling; the usual trip took fourteen days.

At the beginning of 1836 there still was no regular mail service to this outpost. A petition was sent by Henry H. Sibley to Washington in an effort to have a mail route established between Fort Snelling and Prairie du Chien. This was in December, 1835. It took another year until a regular route was established, but it was only the latter half of that year that the Postal Department paid the hired runner.

John Short was hired and was paid by the Army at Fort Snelling; his salary for three months was $48.21-3/4 cents. One might well wonder how this salary was determined at this odd figure. The answer was provided by the financial report of the Post Office. Total receipts for the three months period was $73.39-1/4. The Postmaster was paid on a commission basis; thirty percent of letter postage receipts, fifty percent of newspaper receipts, and two cents each for free or franked letters. The total sum of these three items allowed him $25.18 for three months leaving $48.21-3/4 for the runner.

Even though this route from Prairie du Chien was now an established route, the service had not improved; it seemed impossible as long as the service depended upon runners to bring better service, so it was many years until weekly mail became a reality in Minnesota.

Records of the second quarter of 1837 show that of the total letter postage collected, about seventy-five percent was on unpaid letters mailed from the offices and addresses to Fort Snelling. The sender had the choice of prepaying or allowing the receiver to pay. During this quarter only $17.00 was collected in postal fees. These were seventy free letters mailed, the official correspondence of the Indian Agent, the Fort Commander and the Postmaster.

Twelve years after the Post Office was established at Fort Snelling, the government bought from the Indians the area between the St. Croix and the Mississippi Rivers. Within a year this land was opened for white settlers. The second Post Office was established at Lake St. Croix, later named Point Douglas. This was at the junction of the St. Croix and the Mississippi.

By 1842 another Post Office was established at Kamposia, a Methodist Mission for the Indians near South St. Paul. By 1846, Still-water and St. Paul both were named as Post Offices.

In 1849 the Minnesota Territory was organized taking in that part of Wisconsin Territory between the St. Croix and Mississippi Rivers as well as part of the Iowa Territory from the Mississippi westward to the Missouri River, including much of the Dakota's.

By June the Territory of Minnesota contained eighteen Post Offices, one even up in Pembina. In St. Paul Henry Jackson became the first Postmaster, the Post Office being in his store. This office had an income for the first three months of operation of $3.43. St. Anthony Falls had a Post Office by October 1, 1849.

By 1851 the list included Reeds Landing, Red Wing, Point Douglas, Cottage Grove, Red Rock, Stillwater, Marine Mills, Taylors Falls, Lac Qui Parle, Sauk Rapids, Fort Gaines, Swan River and Long Prairie.

While all this was going on in our new territory surrounding the Fort Snelling area, a natural supply line was springing into life in the northwest. The Selkirks, traders and trappers soon found that the continuous waterway of the Red River and the Minnesota would take them to St. Paul and that trading center easier and faster. Therefore, this soon became an established route carrying all types of supplies and even the mail. As St. Paul expanded and grew the mails from the British settlements, including the Hudson's Fur Trading Company, used this mode for their mail deliveries. These mails were always sent by special messengers as it contained much valuable cash, letters and other mail, all of which was posted at the St. Paul Post Office.

The newspaper, the St. Paul Pioneer of St. Paul, had as of March 6, 1850 as its headline, "Arrival of an express mail from the Red River of the north by dog team in sixteen days." All this heavy mail came from Pembina and the Selkirks. This may have been the last such trip as on May 18, 1850 a Post Office was established at Pembina with Norman W. Kittson as Postmaster. This Post Office eventually replaced St. Paul as the American mailing office for the British Colony. The mail required U.S. postage prepaid by the sender and the Red River settlement Postmaster stamped or wrote the amount of postage on each piece of mail.

Although the first United States postage stamp was issued on July 1, 1847, stamps were as yet not in use in these far-flung areas of our nation; nor were there postal cards, stamped envelopes, parcel post, money orders, special or registered mail available yet.

The Post Office usually occupied the far

corner of a store. The better ones had a pigeonholed box into which the Postmaster placed each patron's mail, but others had a box beneath their store counter. When a patron asked for his mail, the Postmaster merely lifted the box to the top of his wood plank counter, leaving the patron to sort out his own and that of his neighbor or those along the route he would travel upon his return -- this in spite of the great importance placed upon the arrival of regular mail.

William Mitchel of St. Cloud wrote that in 1855 the mail was delivered from St. Paul in a two horse hack. The driver would leave the mailbag at a log hotel at the east bank of the river and anyone coming in helped himself. Usually many came when the news was spread that the mail had arrived.

The residents of Wisconsin displayed even more genuine neighborliness in their mail deliveries. When the mailman came, his first stop was at the hotel. There he dumped all the mail upon a bed where everybody sorted their own and their neighbors, there being no distinction between the Postmaster and the patrons. All were equally interested in whatever news, good or bad, was contained in all this mail after many weeks of no mail.

Finally the day came when roads were being surveyed and laid out. Soon after stage routes were established and mail deliveries were contracted to the stage drivers. This was not always successful as whenever a driver had an urge to lighten the load, he thought little of dumping a sack or two. At times the mail sacks were not even picked up at the station in order to take on more paying passengers. The settlers were still bitterly complaining by the long delays between mail deliveries.

Travel during any season, except when the ground was frozen, was still almost impossible. There were no bridges over streams or rivers and the so-called roads were a bottomless quagmire from spring through fall. In winter the heavy snows and blizzards halted travel for weeks on end while the settlers grumbled and complained. More Post Offices were established, but this only caused more complaining because nothing brought the mail with greater speed or regularity.

Postmasters received much blame, the general opinion being that he was withholding the mail until he had read it all first.

Having a subscription to a newspaper in 1855 was not every man's privilege and receiving a letter through the mail called for a holiday. All the neighbors came to hear what news the letter contained. Sometimes the recipient of the letter could not read it; then the pastor or school teacher was called to read and translate it to all who came to discuss whatever the letter may have contained.

The year when Minnesota became a state, the number of Post Offices jumped from eighteen in 1851 to five hundred in 1859. In some towns the mail came as often as three times per week. The mail, haphazard as it was, played a great part, a most vital part in the development of our state. The information in this article has been gleaned from *The Post Office in Early Minnesota,* by J.W. Patterson and from Minnesota History, Volume 40, Summer 1966 page 78-89 and loaned to me by Minnesota Historical Society. I'm grateful for their help, without it I could not have found much of this information.

CHAPTER IX

Minnesota's Wild Fruits

Wild rice and the cranberry were the most valuable of all the many varieties of wild fruits which were so plentiful in seasons. Wild strawberries, raspberries and cherries were plentiful from spring through fall; blackberries, gooseberries, besides grapes and plums, were in so great abundance that the early settlers brought them into towns where they sold from $.50 to $3.00 per bushel.

The huckleberry and the wild grape were

the most abundant and most freely used by the settler to make his native wine to refresh himself beneath his own fruit bearing tree.

From the cranberry marsh that nearly every homestead had, the settler made more than from his crops during the early years before he had his land cleared from roots and sometimes huge boulders and stones.

U. S. Geologist David Dale reported this, "This native product of Minnesota is nowhere more abundant or of finer quality than in the region bordering on the St. Croix River." There were 256,000 acres of cranberry marsh between the St. Croix and Mississippi Rivers. The price received was between $3.00 and $8.00 per bushel. Geologist Owen suggested that the cranberry section of Minnesota could well be fitted as "homesteads" by producing the cranberry as the main cash crop. He wrote, "The drainage of the cranberry marshes may be so arranged that they may be cleared and all other grasses and weeds eradicated, then restocked with good thrifty vines, care being taken to plant the frost resisting variety. Drainage might be controlled so that the cultivator could irrigate the vines when his experience had taught him to be the proper time. There is a splendid field for some enterprising genius to carry out this suggestion and reap a fortune.

The apple is not native to Minnesota, but the settlers wasted no time before apple trees were planted. It took many years to successfully produce this delicious fruit in our state. The highbush cranberry is a native shrub and successfully grown all over the state, and with but little care has served a succession of generations to this day.

Wild rice -- its botanical name Zizania Aquatica, Pshu of the Sioux, Manimin of the Chippewa. It always has been and still remains as the main staple food for the Indians. It rates high in nutrition and is equally tasty to the white man's family. An acre of rice was considered equal to an acre of wheat.

Geologists estimated that there were 75,000 acres of wild rice in the triangle between the Mississippi, St. Croix and Prairie Rivers. "It is particularly in the lake-like expansions of rivers, toward their sources, which give such marked features to the distribution of these northern streams. Wild rice is rarely met with on inland lakes which have no outlets.

"The rice lakes are most liberally distributed in the sections of the Red Cedar, Nemakagon, St. Croix and Snake Rivers in the south, and the sources of the Big Fork and Red Lake Rivers in the north, and farther east in the Lake Vermillion region. The grain has been frequently introduced to the attention of 'cultivators' as it is worthy of notice; not only for the value of its product, but the peculiar nature of the soil, being unfit for any other cultivated grain.

"As a native of the northwest, it is undoubtedly susceptible for increased production. Wild rice will, before long, constitute as important an element in the wealth of this region as it now does to its native inhabitants.

"Wild rice is probably a biennial yielding greatest in alternate years. It grows from a bed submerged by water from six to twenty inches. One root may have three to ten heads. I observed one fact worthy of attention to any grower. Plants on the margin of the water, left upon the dry ground by receding of the water level were quite as prolific as those in water."

The Indian went into his ripening rice paddy with his canoe; they went in pairs, usually husband and wife. Bending the laden heads over the side of their canoe, they grasped handfuls and beat the kernels out with sticks until the canoe was loaded and the rice was then dumped upon a dry spot on the shore to dry.

After having dried several days in the sun and wind, the rice was further dried or processed in huge iron kettles over outdoor fires, after which it was hulled. For this a pit was dug out of the hard earth of sufficient depth to hold about a half bushel, the pit being first tamped and smoothed until it resembled an earthen bowl. On either side a pole was driven into the earth with another in the center, after which the heated rice was poured into the pit. A man in bare feet then stepped into the pit holding onto the poles to balance himself in so small an area and proceeded to stamp and trample until the hulls were separated from the kernels.

The rice was then removed and winnowed. This was usually done by the women. While standing against a hard blowing wind, she held the vessels high above her head and poured the rice slowly from one vessel into another. The hulls were taken by the wind leaving the clean kernels in her vessels. The rice was then ready for use. To preserve it, the Indian women placed it into baskets made of reeds or bark, covered it and placed it into a dry earth pit where standing water or seepage was unlikely to damage the rice.

The Indian women prepared wild rice in a variety of ways. A favorite recipe called for fish and dried berries along with the rice. She boiled the fish and rice until the bones were tender, after which she added the berries and continued to boil until they too were tender. The bones supplied them with the calcium they needed as well as to add flavor as seasoning, as salt or pepper was unknown to the natives. Salt and condiments as we know them today were not to be obtained by the early settlers living in remote areas. They used dried herbs and roots as seasoning. The food grown on the virgin soil provided them with needed minerals.

CHAPTER X

Transportation-Navigation-Railroads

In the year 1849 Captain Pope wrote in his official report, "I believe that Lake Superior, the Mississippi and other rivers, and our railroads bring us as near to the eastern and southern markets as any other state, mainly Iowa, Illinois or Wisconsin. I regard it as not at all difficult to deliver the produce of this whole country at the western extremity of Lake Superior than it is to deliver the produce of the interior of Wisconsin or Illinois to any point on Lake Michigan."

"The distance from Buffalo, New York to Chicago is less than to Fond du Lac; in open steamboat, navigation would be of little consequence."

"This line of railroad, therefore, to connect the head of navigation of the Red River of the north with Lake Superior could be easily built by the appropriation of the alternate grants of lands. This would enable Minnesota to compete in the eastern markets with Illinois and Wisconsin. The second route from the head of navigation of the Red River to the head of navigation of the St. Peter's River would open the valleys of the Red River and the St. Peter's to the Mississippi below the falls of St. Anthony."

Another report of Captain Pope's on water communication states, "The peculiar conformation of the whole region of country between the Minnesota, Mississippi and the head of navigation of the Red River of the north and the water communications is remarkable; not only for their great number, but for their almost unlimited extent. This will enable the farmer and manufacturer to transport to Lake Superior or the Mississippi all his supplies, produce and articles of manufacture in one-fourth the time and at one-twentieth the cost that the same could be carted from the interior of Illinois, Iowa or Wisconsin to any navigable stream.

"In point of time and expense (the two great considerations), Minnesota has equal advantages with interior parts of the other three states."

"As to navigable rivers -- A steamboat on Leech Lake already traverses 300 miles on the waters of the upper Mississippi, another plies its vacation on Lake Minnetonka. The steamer International runs from Fort Abercrombie to Fort Gary on the Red River. Four daily lines employ sixty-one steamboats and barges on the lower Mississippi, the Minnesota and the St. Croix."

In a report written by General R. K. Warren, he recommended the improvement of the Fox and Wisconsin Rivers so as to connect the Mississippi River with Lake Michigan. "It is safe to say we believe that a good line of water transportation from the Mississippi to Green Bay can be so built as to profitably transport at one-half cent per ton per mile. The line would be two hundred and eighty miles long. This would make the cost of the entire distance $1.40 per ton, a saving of $1.90 per ton upon the cheapest railroad transportation.

"On our present wheat crop this would save $31.40 per ton. In the aggregate, three million seven hundred eighty thousand dollars."

This improvement was urged by the legislatures of Iowa, Wisconsin, Minnesota and by a Canal Convention held at Prairie du Chien in November 1868.

In the governor's message of January 1869 he stated, "It is ascertained from reports and tables carefully prepared that the average net costs of a ton per mile is eighteen mills. It has also been ascertained that the average net cost by canal is from four to six mills, showing that the cost of transportation by canal is about one-third of that by rail. In the meantime, while this improvement is yet to be secured, we have already Lake Superior almost connected with the

Mississippi by rail."

"LAKE SUPERIOR SAVES US 882 MILES and brings us as near to New York market as Chicago," so were the headlines of the day. Mr. Wheeler wrote in his official report of 1861, "The St. Paul and Superior Railroad being now virtually an accomplished fact, its bonds amount to $4,500,000 having been cashed and its construction to be finished by 1870.

"In my former report it was shown by an analysis of the comparative cost of transportation by water and railroad that the frontage of Minnesota on Lake Superior is equivalent, in a commercial sense, to a decrease of the distance from New York measured upon railroad lines of 882 miles. That is to say, the difference in the cost of transportation in favor of the water route would pay the freight upon her products from her districts for that distance.

"In other words, her water communications place her interior districts near par commercially with states depending upon railroad outlets; for example the southwestern Pennsylvania and the upper Ohio valley. By this channel, therefore, when Minnesota shall have built a railroad to Lake Superior, it will cost no more to ship a bushel of wheat from Redwing as from Pittsburg. But, to compare the commercial effect of this position with other states having a frontage on the lakes, the result is quite as favorable to Minnesota.

"A vessel on her way from Buffalo to Chicago for a load of grain at a distance of sixty miles before she enters the Straits of Mackinac is at the entrance of Lake Superior and almost as near Fond du Lac as Chicago. The distance from New York to Fond du Lac is 1,510 miles, or only 85 miles farther, an inappreciable difference in transportation by water; so that as an absolute fact, Minnesota is as near to New York by water as Illinois."

Unfortunately for our young state these grand dreams did not all materialize; the railroads which were built were not for the convenience of the settlers, although the land had all been given free for these purposes.

The enthusiasm of the people was matched by the flattering and encouraging words by promoters and officials up and down the country. Glowing speeches were spread throughout the land.

"All this land has been shut out from the knowledge of the world. A new era is at hand. The people of the Atlantic are wooing the people of the Pacific; they would all be united by an iron band.

"Starting from La Crosse to St. Paul, Minnesota, from Fond du Lac at the head of Lake Superior, and from St. Paul we have a system of railroads which are partly built and which are now under construction to the Red River of the north. Carrying out a project of a railroad to the Pacific at whatever the cost to the people and the future of this country will present a panorama of magnificence unexampled in history, of which the splendor of Roman wealth in the days of Augustus will sink into insignificance."

"The silks, teas and opium of China will swiftly speed over the Rocky Mountains to the warehouses of Europe. The spices and oriental luxuries of India will be transported over lands where the red race but an age since has trapped the beaver and the ermine. The reawakened commerce of Japan would find across the prairie land of Hudson Bay's territory the gold of California, of British Columbia, and the Saskatchewan valley would find a safe passage by the Great Lakes to the Atlantic

"The wool of California would find a direct route to England. The homeward and outward bound would cross the Atlantic on their way to India, Australia, California, British Columbia, North America and the United States in social companionship."

The Northern Route -- the shortest and most available, its effect upon Minnesota as taken from Governor Marshall's message of January 1869 -- "The applicability of this glowing language to Minnesota becomes apparent when we consider that Minnesota becomes the mouth of the funnel through which all this traffic must pass, where bulk must be broken and cars changed.

"The single fact which fixes this destiny and crystallizes it as a logical conclusion may be seen in the following figures. The distance from New York to Puget Sound via the Northern Pacific Railroad is 2,892 miles. From New York to San Francisco via the Union Pacific Railroad 3,417 miles. A difference of 525 miles in favor of The Northern Route. From Chicago to San Francisco by the Union Pacific road the distance is 2,448 miles. From the west end of Lake Superior to Puget Sound by the Northern Pacific route the distance is 1,775 miles, or more than one-fourth. While Puget Sound is nearer by from 700 to 1,000 miles to Japan, China and India than San Francisco is."

The Chicago Tribune admits the superiority of the northern route with these words taken from their paper. "If the company builds the road in good faith, they will become the largest landed proprietors in the world. Congress has granted them every second section for forty miles on each side of it from the head of Lake Superior to Puget Sound or the Pacific Ocean, a belt of country west from Lake Superior entirely across the continent for forty miles.

"The distance is in round numbers 1,700 miles, in all 68,000 square miles, territory enough to make three states as large as Illinois, Massachusetts and Connecticut. Nor is this worthless, like nine-tenths of that along the Union Pacific Railways. Surveys and the accounts of all travelers agree that the country along nearly all the entire line of this road is capable of cultivation and sustaining a large population."

The word to go forward. The Philadelphia Press of May 22, 1869 wrote the following concerning this venture. "Mr. Ogden, in his speech at the Cooper Institute said he had been engaged for the past two weeks in negotiating with JAY COOKE & COMPANY OF PHILADELPHIA by which Mr. Cooke would become the financial agent for the construction of the Great Northern Railroad from Lake Superior through Minnesota and across the plains to Columbia River, bringing us 800 miles nearer to the Empire of Japan than the present Pacific Railroad.

"The negotiation was substantially closed and most satisfactorily too. He hoped the work would soon be commenced and completed."

"This is a deserved tribute to the financial ability of Mr. Cooke and no less to the business reputation of Philadelphia. The new road which is to run from Lake Superior to Puget Sound will probably in the end be the Great Continental Railway, on account of the advantages it possesses of being projected across the continent on the isogeothermal line which secures at all seasons of the year a mild climate which in turn secures wood and water."

Surveys had been going on and an expedition was sent on foot by Jay Cooke to examine the entire route. Carlton was the Boston correspondent of this expedition and sent the following report from the Otter Tail country. "We have met a long train of wagons filled with immigrants who have come from Wisconsin, Illinois, Indiana and Ohio to make their homes in this fertile valley.

"A crate with chickens or a few pigs

underneath each and every wagon, a cow or two tied behind the wagon or grazing on the luscious grass with the growing boys and girls herding them along.

"Not only on this road, but In every section of the state we behold such scenes. The advance is all along the line, towns and villages are springing up as if by magic. Every day adds thousands of acres to those already in cultivation, the wheat fields of this year are much wider than they were the year before. This year the population has increased nearly by 100,000. No wonder the world is coming to Minnesota, where under healthier skies can a farm be had for the taking?

"The news from our State Exchanges and from the highways and byways is that we have a flood tide of immigration, thanks to the efforts of Colonel Mattson, our State Immigration Agent, who has been on a visit of months to his native Sweden, and to the documents sown abroad by the wise and liberal provisions of our legislature.

"The Scandinavian swarms of the north, the hardy Germans of central Europe and the sons of the Free Isle all are rushing, filled with eagerness and hope to the free homesteads and healthy climate."

As a result of this increase of landowners, the population jumped from 50,000 in 1864 to 73,000 in 1869. Land held by individuals aside from homestead claims was 11,000,000 acres. By homestead entry the acreage was 356,876 by 1869. Number of dwelling houses were 70,000.

The Governor's message of January 1869 contained this encouraging message. "I rejoice to be able to inform you that the Northern Pacific Railroad Company has effected an arrangement with the ablest parties in the country for the construction of the road. A telegram of the fourth of January informs me that work will probably commence in February."

The condition of our railroads was at that time:

	In operation
First division St. Paul & Pacific mail line	51 miles

First division St. Paul & Pacific to Sauk Rapids	81 miles
Minnesota Valley to St. Paul & Sioux City	90 miles
Milwaukee, St. Paul & Minneapolis	131 miles
Winona & St. Peter	106 miles
Southern Minnesota	50 miles
Lake Superior & Mississippi	30 miles
Hastings & Dakota	20 miles

The state had a total of 559 miles of railroad in operation by January 1, 1869.

The governor's message continued, "Each of the ten roads named have a Congressional Land Grant of 6,400 acres for each mile of road, except the North Pacific which has 12,800 acres to the mile. In addition to this the Lake Superior and Mississippi Railroad has a grant of seven sections to the mile of state lands, and a $250,000 bonus of St. Paul city bonds.

"First, the St. Paul & Pacific R.R. from St. Paul via St. Anthony, Sauk Rapids and Crow Wing to Pembina on the Red River, 400 miles.

"Second, first division of St. Paul & Pacific main line from St. Paul via St. Anthony and Minneapolis to Breckenridge on the Red River, 200 miles. Also from St. Paul via St. Anthony to Sauk Rapids, 81 miles; with a branch to Lake Superior between Sauk Rapids and Crow Wing, 120 miles.

"Third, St. Paul & Sioux City (later named Minnesota Valley) from St. Paul via Mankato to the south western border of the state, 170 miles; to connect with the road from Sioux City, 70 miles.

"Fourth, the Milwaukee, St. Paul & Minneapolis from St. Paul and Minneapolis via Mendota, Faribault and Owatonna to the state line nearly due south; intersects the Winona & St. Peter at Owatonna and gives the only all rail route to Milwaukee and Chicago.

"Fifth, Lake Superior & Mississippi from St. Paul nearly north to Duluth with authority to connect to Superior, 150 miles."

"Sixth, the Hastings & Dakota from Hastings via Farntington through the counties of Scott, Carver and McLeod to Big Stone Lake, no mileage available.

"Seventh, the Winona & St. Peter from Winona via Owatonna, Waseca and St. Peter to the western boundary, 250 miles.

"Eighth, the Southern Minnesota R.R. from La Crescent up the Root River valley through the entire section of counties via Lanesboro, Austin, Albert Lea, Winnebago City, Fairmont and Jackson to the state line, 250 miles; thence to the great bend of the Missouri.

"Ninth, the Northern Pacific Railroad from

Lake Superior, either at Superior or Bayfield via St. Cloud or Crow Wing to Breckenridge. The line has not definitely been established although two surveys have been made."

"Tenth, the Stillwater & St. Paul via White Bear Lake, 20 miles.

"Eleventh, the Chicago & St. Paul Railroad from St. Paul via Hastings and other river towns having a grant of state lands fourteen sections per mile and graded, 20 miles."

CHAPTER XI

Education And Religion - Schools

After Minnesota had achieved statehood the new legislature provided two sections in each township to belong to the school fund, making it in the aggregate about 3,000,000 acres after surveying to sell at not less than $5.00 per acre. The cash proceeds being invested in United States and Minnesota State bonds.

The sales of school lands during the year had been 79,910 acres producing $64,840.61, which had added to the previous monies of the permanent school fund and made the magnificent sum of two million, seventy-five thousand and eighty-two dollars.

Interest of the school fund for 1868 was $115,794.38. A two mill tax was levied in each county for school purposes. Number of children in the state between five and twenty-one were 129,131, an increase of 14,682 over 1867.

Teachers numbered 3,276, an increase of 621. Teachers were paid $322,785.00, an increase of $67,798.00. Value of school houses was $1,091,559.42, an increase of $345,168.37. Value of school houses built in 1868 was $288,178.37. Number of school houses were 1,000 frame, 37 brick, 48 stone, 61 log, or a total of 1,766 school houses costing approximately $1,500,000. These provisions were more liberal than that of any other state in the Union.

In 1868 the State University with a fine, costly building, an endowment of 46,080 acres of land, besides 120,000 acres of agricultural college land, and a full corps of professors was in successful operation at St. Anthony without expense to students except for board. The University was an experimental farm for instruction in scientific farming and was to be free from any denominational influences.

During that same year Normal Schools were in operation at Winona, Mankato and another soon to be opened at St. Cloud. There was also a Catholic School at Clinton in Stearns County, a Methodist College at Red Wing, a Congregational College at Northfield, an Episcopal College at Faribault. Commercial Colleges were at St. Paul and at Minneapolis, besides other classical academies and female seminaries.

Catholic churches in the state numbered 123 in 1868 and were valued at $500,000 with a membership of 120,000, including baptized children and 60 priests.

Methodists had 65 churches valued at $228,550. There were 8,229 members, 108 ministers, including 10 Scandinavians. The German Methodists had 35 churches valued at $54,000, with a membership of 2,834 and 28 ministers.

Episcopalians had 28 churches valued at

$204,850 with 1,720 members and 30 ministers. No valuation was stated on the Baptists who had 27 churches with 4,210 members, nor on the Congregationals who had 67 congregations with 2,624 members and 52 ministers.

Presbyterians had 45 churches valued at $100,000; 2,156 members and 40 ministers (New School). Presbyterians of the Old School had 48 churches, 1,384 members and 33 ministers.

Lutherans had 79 congregations, nearly 6,000 members, 43 German ministers and 2 English ministers. The Swedish Lutherans had 19 churches with 3,250 members and 9 ministers.

Universalists had 20 churches with 900 members and 12 ministers. There were also Adventists, Swedenborgians, Cambell Baptists and Spirituals.

Far in advance of the building of churches services were conducted in the homes of the pioneers served by traveling ministers and missionaries. During pleasant summer weather it was not unusual for the parishioners to gather beneath the shade of spreading tree branches. They brought their lunches and any musical instruments they may have had so that after the services the day was spent in visiting, playing games and singing. Marriages were performed and children were baptized because another service might not be held until the following year.

Missions Among The Native Indians

The following is a condensation from the report of Doctor A. Branard, a resident surgeon at the Chippewa Agency at White Earth Reservation, who credits Reverend J. G. Wright as twenty years a missionary and government teacher of manual labor for Indian children at Leech Lake.

"From 1833 to 1862 The American Board of Missions have labored among the Chippewas, since then they have abandoned them. Reverend F. Ayer began in 1833, labored seven years at Sand Point Lake and quit. Reverend Mr. Boutwell followed in 1835, remained for four years and quit. In 1840 Reverend Mr. Spetes of the Methodist Church tried it but became discouraged and left. In 1853 Reverend Mr. Breck of the Episcopal Church struck in vigorously at Gull Lake and Leech Lake, erected several large buildings during his eighteen months there but also left."

Dr. Branard, with the help of two others, went to Red Wing where conditions looked favorable. Here the NOBLE RED MAN was still much in evidence. They produced good crops of corn and potatoes and they were a peaceful, happy people. There was less evidence of whiskey brought in by the Voyageurs and foreigners. Work here continued until 1859 when it too was abandoned.

The constant complaints of these worthy gentlemen was that the traders and Voyageurs used whiskey to trade with the Indians. Suspicion of the missionary was instilled into the minds of the natives by those in high offices and even by those hired and paid by the government. Their conduct was notorious, no effort was made by those who had authority to suppress this traffic.

Their immoral control was revolting to the natives who desired to keep away from any and all white men.

At Gull and Leech Lakes no less than $30,000 was spent, in addition to the free missionary labors, with about the same results as at other places. While there were individual instances of conversions, the adverse influences to the success of the missions were increased in strength.

Catholic Missions - The Reverend John Ireland of St. Paul stated the following in his account. "The Jesuits have extensive missions from Grant Portage, the extreme northeastern boundary of Minnesota, to the far northwest in British America; their principal station is at Fort Williams."

"Reverend John Chebus of Bayfield- has an Indian mission at Fond du Lac, Minnesota; Joseph Buh and Ignatius Tomazin at Crow Wing, from whence they make regular visits to the Indians at Mille Lac, Oak Point, Leech Lake, Red Lake, Winnebigoshish and White Earth Reservations. At all these places we have baptized Indians.

"There is an excellent church edifice at Grand Portage exclusively for Indians and a school opened this month (October 1869) at White Oak Point. As to the general prospects of the Indian missions in Minnesota, our priests express themselves in no way discouraged."

Undoubtedly these early missionaries were hard working, courageous gentlemen. When possible they traveled on horseback to the far flung frontier. More often they mushed through the snow and mud on foot carrying their bedroll, medications and items required to conduct services, on their backs .

Reverend Francis X. Pierz was one such missionary, German speaking, an immigrant from Austria, he soon learned the difficult Indian dialects, which must have been the key to his success in the Indian villages. He was loved by all.

Besides his strenuous work among the Indians, he was in charge of all the people within a radius of no less than a hundred miles. The farthest ones were reached semi-annually at irregular intervals. When he arrived within the vicinity of his destination, he would pause to send out smoke signals. Thereafter, everyone informed their neighbor that Father Pierz was due here for the approaching feast day.

Without fail, when he would arrive he was always welcomed by a crowd of white and red men alike who had come on foot the same as he had. Indians and whites mingled as one at these gatherings to hear once again the word of God from the lips of this God fearing lovable man.

Father Francis X. Pierz had founded three churches by 1867; one at Rush Lake, Ottertail City, one at Rich Prairie (now Pierz named in his honor), and one at Prairie d St. Marie, 0' Chippewa (now Millerville). All are flourishing parishes today.

The Benedictines have been in central Minnesota since 1857. They came as German-speaking missionaries to Stearns County where they were the founders of St. John's Community. The first missionaries were Abbot Rupert Seidenbush with six other young men all ordained as missionaries. They traveled extensively all over the upper one-half of Minnesota and Dakota territories to teach, and brought the word of God to as many as 25,000 red men and 15,000 new settlers.

CHAPTER XII

Life in the Pineries

By February 1869 Captain John P. Owens, who had been a resident of Minnesota for twenty years, estimated that a billion feet of timber had already been cut. Alarm was felt regarding the future needs of the state unless this continuous harvesting be curbed. Estimates by old pine land explorers varied from three to eight times that amount still standing. A mean estimate was made to bring it to five and one-half billion feet still remaining.

The average annual cutting of one hundred million feet would exhaust the St. Croix Pineries within fifty years. Two percent of growth would extend the measure to one hundred years. Captain Owens comments, "It must be remembered that tracts of which all suitable timber was cut ten years ago is now about ready to be cut again, so rapid is the growth of the pine tree in Minnesota. A man who owns pine land may, as a general rule, calculate that it is gaining by ten percent annually by growth."

GOING IN, by H. M. Atkins, Princeton, Minnesota, "In November the crews and teams start into the woods. Large, strong wagons are drawn by two, four or six horses, or six to eight oxen to each wagon heavily laden with supplies, which means all the necessities plus some luxuries for the support of the men and feed for horses and oxen.

"The teams are handled by crews of men who are to cut the trees and prepare the logs. They wind their way among the pine trees of the St. Croix, the Rum and the upper Mississippi Rivers. The land has been previously explored and having arrived at the selected spot, the work of building a camp for the men and a stable for the teams is begun.

"The lumber men are not always the owners of the land, but usually buy the stumpage at a specified price per thousand feet, the amount being ascertained by 'scaling' or measuring after the logs are cut. The amount paid for stumpage varies from $1.00 to $3.00 per thousand feet according to the quality of the trees and the distance from streams of drivable waters.

"The men become quite expert in the job of managing logs. They may stand erect on one and keep on their feet while the log rolls over and over in the rapid current, with no other aid except a pick hand spike seven or eight feet long. The lumberjacks find great humor in an occasional slip when the man loses his footing and 'pulls the hole in behind him'. Then great is the amusement among his associates.

"The aim is to keep the logs moving continually and are so numerous as to hide the waters for miles at times. It is late June before they are all safely 'boomed' into the vicinity of large mills for manufacturing into lumber for distribution far and near.

"Camp life is not all hard work. Sundays are always free to be spent in games, music, reading and gambling. Teamsters receive $40 to $50 per month, cooks $40, foremen $80 to $100, good hoppers $35 to $40, swampers $30, and ordinary hands $20 to $25 per month. Wages on rafts averaged $25 per month, pilots $1,200 to $2,000 per season.

"The average price of logs at Stillwater in 1868-9 was $22 per thousand. Two hundred and twenty-five rafts left Stillwater in 1868 with each raft requiring twenty-five men to run it, giving employment to five hundred men.

"The men on the logs are continually wet and no Sundays are observed. It is demanding and exhausting work but demands the highest wages, $2.00 to $5.00 per day plus board. From dawn until dark the men spend their day in icy cold water for the logs must be kept moving to prevent continually forming jams in the swift currents.

"The men are organized in crews of various sizes according to the number of logs to be managed, each crew having a boss driver as a leader. A tent of sufficient size to shelter the men while sleeping on the ground wrapped in wool blankets and quilts goes with each crew to the river.

"A batteau, which is a long sharp boat, and a wongin, which is a large clumsy flat boat for supplies, also follows the crew. The cook moves along from day to day with the batteau and the wongin as the meals, except morning and evening, are taken to the men five times each day. At all times are the men well fed.

"If the water is very high, the cross currents carry many logs over low places and into the banks, sloughs and gullies. The work of moving them back into the stream is extremely hard and demanding and is called 'sacking'. The men must stand in ice water up to their waists at times, and with the aid of picks and 'cant-dogs' get them moving back.

"The main camp where the men live over

the winter is usually placed near a river or stream for convenience in water supplies, the material is always nearby. The main building is a large and well-built log house with roof of pine or oak. Shingles are made of splits. The floor is of boards of small pine hewed flat and smooth. It's heated by a large box stove at one end of the camp while a huge cook stove, which is managed by the cook, is on the far side of the camp. A large board table is the only fixture in the building. Dishes are of tin instead of crockery.

"Along one end, or if the crew is large, along both sides are the bunks. These are shelves elevated a foot or two above the floor, six to seven feet wide, and as long as the length of the camp will allow. Along one side of the bunks, planks are positioned to form a box-like frame to hold the marsh hay, which is piled into this box which forms the bunks. A foot or more in length than the box is a heavy quilt-like spread which covers all the hay. The men lie with their heads to the wall, feet towards the stove. Another heavy comforter is used to cover the men.

"Clothing is never removed except for their

boots. This boxlike frame accommodates from forty to sixty men all sleeping in one bed. Benches made of the same crude unfinished lumber are near the tables. Kerosene lamps are used for lighting."

"The stables are far better than the camp for the men, as they are well 'chinked' so no drafts can enter. The teams are well cared for and fed with choice hay, made in season the summer before, and unground oats with wheat, corn and barley ground.

"Long before daybreak the cook and the teamsters are up to prepare for an early start. All hands are called for breakfast. No man ever shaved and what washing was done was done in ice cold water in a tin bucket outside the building. After the meal all hands, except the cook, went off to their work in the timber. The food, however, is always good and plentiful. The men receive good wages, so rarely complain. Every man knows his job and usually is well qualified to do a days work.

"The choppers chop down the trees and

trim the branches and the tops. The sled tenders clear the debris around the trees' trunk and apply ropes and tackles or chains for loading. The sawyers are the most important men in the crew as they cut with sharp axes the symbols, letters and signs which constitute the owner's recorded mark and by which each log may be identified wherever it ends up.

"The swampers are in charge of the trails, clearing them of undergrowth for the teamsters who do the hauling and managing the teams. Bobsleds, long and wide, are used for hauling and are low to make loading possible. With tackles and chains they are hauled to the landing, this being on the river or stream clear of all timber, usually on a steep bank, and are left there waiting for the spring waters to float them to their destination.

"The men work until noon and then return to camp for their well-earned dinner, after which they return to work until dark and then return to camp for supper. After supper they amuse themselves usually by playing cards.

"The job is over when the spring warmth melts the snow. The hardest of hard work begins then when the rivers begin their spring flowing. The great piles of logs at all the landings are rolled down into the flowing waters and set afloat. These men are called the river drivers.

CHAPTER XIII

Life and the Staff of Life are the Chief Productions in Minnesota

This glorious tribute to our young state came from Ohio and was taken from the Cincinnati Times in 1865. "Health and wheat are the first attractions in this upper state. While the wheat crop has been subject to many vicissitudes in other states, it has steadily kept up in the young and promising state of Minnesota." The yield of wheat in Minnesota in 1864 was twenty-five bushels per acre.

Here is another tribute from the State of Illinois, or rather from Washington, D.C., as it was from no less than the President himself, ABRAHAN LINCOLN, in 1859. At an address delivered at the Wisconsin Agricultural Fair he said, "The best result of all the testimony I was able to collect is that the average wheat yield in Illinois was not over eight bushels per acre. Iowa in 1849 produced fourteen bushels, While the largest known crop in Ohio in 1850 was twelve bushels. Minnesota, the banner state, produced an average of twenty-one bushels.

"While these are the average yields, it is but fair to say that thirty and forty bushels are frequently raised. Especially this is true of winter wheat, and it is also proper to say that Minnesota had a lot lower acreage than she should have on account of the great number of slouchy, unskilled tillers of the soil who are not farmers but only men who moved west.

"Shallow plowing, irregular sowing, deficient harrowing, careless and wasteful harvesting, together with too much reliance upon the rich soil and too little upon cultivation, rotation of crops and seed are evils a thousand fold multiplied over that of in older states.

"To excel them all, even with these drawbacks, is a vindication of Minnesota's agricultural capacity."

"Wintering stock sheds built of straw are generally used by farmers as all stock thrives better by protection during the cold snaps. This is no more true in Minnesota than elsewhere, although the dryness of the climate makes it a little more necessary to house stock than in milder, chillier latitudes. Except for working stock, sheep and hogs, stock are wintered on hay, straw and fodder. Working cattle are fed on turnips and rutabagas, occasionally a little corn.

"Rutabagas are raised on sod or old land, planted as late as July 12th. Some yields as high as 600 to 1,000 bushels per acre. Corn fodder is raised by sowing the corn broadcast or drilling and from either eight to ten tons may be gathered. Clover, timothy and blue grass flourish and the best of the blue joint grows on the prairies without culture. Here the land is free, pasturage free, the running streams and lakes are free. Hay is free or costing only $1.00 to $1.50 per ton, for the use of a new patented mower he may average two tons per acre.

Such was the advertising sent out by promoters into every state. High prices may be obtained as all the forts must be supplied and the growing and ever-coming immigration keep prices high. Beef on the foot ranges from five to eight cents, oxen $25.00 to $175.00 per yoke, and horses $100.00 to $300.00 each. Hogs were ten to thirteen cents dressed. Sheep and wool was temporarily set back by unfriendly legislation.

Dairy business - cheese wholesaling is at fifteen to twenty cents per pound and butter is thirty to forty-five cents. The same abundance of free grass and pure water makes this a profitable branch of husbandry. Minnesota farmers estimate the cost of keeping a cow at $12.50 per year. Her milk at three hundred gallons is equivalent to thirty pounds of cheese and the whey and butter at $10.00.

Good cows in the spring are worth $30.00 to $45.00. There are already a number of large dairy establishments in the state and more preparing to begin. A gentleman from England had bought 40,000 acres near Rush Lake. He is Mr. Thomas W. Wimsley and he says his purpose is to import cattle and sheep of the best blood to stock his farm. If the dairy cow is destined to be the leading interest of northeastern Minnesota, we can readily anticipate a dense and permanent population.

CHAPTER XIV

Bonanza Farming -
Capitalists Turning Farmers

Pennock Pusey, Assistant Secretary of State, wrote as follows about the Oliver Dalrymple estate, about twenty miles from St. Paul. "On three farms of 2,000 acres, 1,700 are in wheat. His yield in 1867 was 35,750 bushels, gross price was $55,550 and profits were $14,500. His profits would have been bigger except for the extremely high prices of 1866; seed costing $2.50 per bushel, with corresponding costs of land breaking and other expenses. These expenses included interest on capital employed in land and otherwise."

"The original cost of the land was $12.00 per acre. After allowing amply for the expenses of building, fencing and other improvements the net on two years crops are more than sufficient to cover the whole, while the market value of the land and improvements have nearly doubled .'

Mr. Dalrymple employed a hundred men and a hundred horses in harvesting and threshing his crop. He had demonstrated the wealth and value of Minnesota land and the fact that capital and business ability can be successfully employed."

About the J. M. Paxton mammoth farm located near Redwood, the St. Paul Dispatch wrote this. "Mr. Paxton's farm lies far up in the Minnesota valley. It consists of 8,000 acres of which 1,000 are now under cultivation. It has been decided to break the entire farm as soon as possible. Mr. Paxton has, all told, upward to 15,000 acres with enough timber to give each purchaser a sufficient tract of woodland to supply his demand for building and fencing. Mr. Paxton has prepared to set out soft maples and cottonwood groves on different parts of his land which, in the course of five to six years, will afford excellent protection against the wintry blasts.

"From the valley of Minnesota he is having a large quantity of maple seeds gathered with which to plant the low and meadow lands. He is also preparing to build a large number of farm buildings on his premises to let to persons desiring to cultivate portions on shares. This will be a great convenience to persons of limited means. This way any person can soon acquire sufficient capital to equip his own farm soon. Having come this far they may select their own claims elsewhere if they so desire.

"The Honorable Clark W. Thompson, the Southern Railway, has a farm of 9,000 acres in one body near Wells in Faribault County which he is dividing into farms of 160 acres each. He has built a brick house on each with 100 acres broke and fenced to be leased on such terms to make it an object to them to abandon the idea of going out west to file on a homestead claim.

"Governor Marshall and Major J. M. Donaldson have a farm of 2,200 acres in Mower County with 100 acres in wheat. They have also made a large purchase in St. Cloud.

"Mr. S. Jenkins' farm, near Lakeville in Dakota County, containing 2,000 acres was offered with the growing crop and all machinery for $40,000."

Profits on small farms demonstrate that one does not need huge capital to own a farm. Mr. Jonas Burell, a small farm owner, gave his account. "In general, farmers pretend to cultivate a large number of acres with as much ease as he can a smaller farm. But in that he is much mistaken, as there will be a general neglect in the build-up of the soil by giving it plenty of manure and thereby enriching its qualities. From ten acres I have raised 318 bushels of number one wheat, from four acres 260 bushels of oats, from five acres 592 bushels of corn, and sixty bushels of carrots from five rods of soil one rod wide.

"Mr. Peter Legro came from Stearns County with $100, a wife and five children to an eighty acre claim. He brought with him all his worldly goods consisting of a gogon plow, one ox and a hard winter ahead of him. Within a few years he had built it up to the extent that it was now $5,000. He was now an independent man."

"Cost and profit of raising wheat in 1868 in Minnesota on forty acres as estimated by this economical farmer - Plowing per acre $1.50, seed at $2.00 per acre per seeding, hand and team five acres per day $3.00, reaping $1.00, binding and setting $3.50, six hands six days at $3.00, $3.00 for board, stacking $1.12-1/2, two hands and team six days help for threshing $1.35, (eight hands two days two span of horses, extra) board of hands and teams two days. Threshing machine expense $1.00 (five cents per bushel). Total cost per acre $11.02, value of products $25.00, profit per acre $13.98. Good wages for the farmer and his team. The price is the average for the past five years."

This is how some cashed in on their homestead rights. The St. Cloud Journal wrote,

"Mr. J. A. Caller of the Minnesota House, some sixteen miles in the timber, put up a shanty costing him $100. That same spring he sold his 'rights' for $600. This man apparently was no homesteader and realized it. Five years of tenancy was required to prove ownership. This took courage and the capacity to face up to the hardship with plentiful measure of humor."

CHAPTER XV

The Great Racial Clash Of 1862

This was undoubtedly the unhappiest, most traumatic experience of our state up to the present day. The settlers, believing that the government had given full satisfaction to the Indians, came here with their families and all worldly belongings to found a new home. They expected to work hard and do without for many years to come, but the only dangers they foresaw were from the wild beasts and animals of which there were many still in abundance.

Bravely the men marched off to defend our nation from an unknown enemy when a soldier on horseback brought him the summons to come along with his musket to report for duty within 36-48 hours. The very young and the aged men were left to care for the new homesteads. Mothers with small children, some still unborn, were left to fend for themselves while their husbands were called to arms in the Civil War. They were easy prey for the restless Sioux braves who had decided that this was a good time to recover the lands their elders had so carelessly sold to the white man. Grievances were easy to find for the Sioux. They were not receiving their payments from the Federal Government because the traders received their shares first, which was the greater share of these monies, claiming the Indians owed them this for supplies they had given them.

In the treaties of Traverse des Sioux and Mendota signed in 1851, the U. S. Government took most of the southern part of what is now our state from the Dakota Indians leaving them only a narrow strip of reservation on each side of the Minnesota River. Twenty-four million acres changed hands in these treaties. Although the Indians had agreed to the deals, they could not comprehend the immensity of their deeds until they were confined to the limitations of the reservation.

Homes were built for them and crude agricultural implements were supplied, which were equal to anything the white settlers had at the time, but the Indians were unhappy in this new arrangement all of which was accomplished by the white man.

In 1858 half of the remaining land was taken by the Federal Government, but the money was never handled by the Dakota Indians. Again, it was the traders who received theirs first, which was the greater part. The Indians were in dire need while the money which did trickle in was delayed for too long periods of time.

With the defeat of the Sioux, the strife came to an end with the battle at Wood Lake. Although the war lasted but six weeks, the damage to both sides was heavy. Many of the Sioux fled west into the plains, some surrendered, while the nonparticipating peaceful Indians, not knowing what to do and fearful of the white man's vengeance, did the same.

Within the year the Dakotas, along with the peaceful Winnebagoes, were rounded up and placed into a poor area where many sickened and died of disease and starvation. Later they were again rounded up and placed into an area just as poor. At long last those who survived were allowed to go to a better area in the Niobrara River Valley of Nebraska.

Attempts of restitution have been made over the years but this scar, which rests upon the white man, will never be erased. Long before the white man came to this continent the Indian tilled the soil. They taught the colonists how to plant, fertilize, harvest and store their crops. They also taught the white man how to preserve the fertility of the soil for all generations to come. But the greedy white man paid no heed of this, instead he wanted all the land and all the profit at once. Therefore, the virgin soil was soon depleted, our forests gone even though much of this replaces itself if given a chance. They gave no consideration for the future of our young state and its sons and daughters who were expected to create a land of plenty for all future generations.

The trauma of the uprising remained for many years. As time went on, the Sioux Indians, homesick and lonely for their native Minnesota, returned in small groups. The white settlers were in deathly fear of them although they harmed no one and wanted only to be left alone and live their lives as their forefathers had.

It is logical to believe that the language barrier caused many a misunderstanding. In this way the white man had the advantage and used it to arouse the anger of the Indian.

Barely was Minnesota of sufficient strength to achieve territorial rights but that the southern slave holders attempted to introduce slavery into the north hoping to make the Indian their slave as they had successfully done to the negro. They had much to learn in this regard.

In the election of 1852 the slave states

triumphed and had renewed their claims that slave property was legitimate in all territories of the United States. This claim was bitterly opposed by Governor Sibley and Henry M. Rice. In 1855 after the annexation of Texas and New Mexico to the Union, the slave holders made another attempt. Some holders even brought negroes into the territory but they could not adjust to our harsh climate, nor could they live peacefully with the Indians or the soldiers. Some remained here, however, and lived among the white settlers and died there. An early grave marker in an old cemetary reads, "Here lies John Doe, he was a negro". Although all else has been obliterated by the ravages of time, this sentence remains bright and clear after more than 125 years.

A leading party in the anti slavery move- ment was a Kentuckian, William R. Marshall of St. Paul, a resident since 1847 and a lover of justice and freedom for all. His anti-slavery work was invaluable to the northern cause.

The novel, *Uncle Tom's Cabin,* by Harriet Beecher Stowe was published in 1852, alerted all to the danger and helped to destroy the last visages of this evil attempt in Minnesota.

Had the southern slave holders remained in their own states, the issue may never have reached the stage of a Civil War.

CHAPTER XVI

The Native Neighbors

The atrocities of the uprising were not easily forgotten and the following is an example of one massacre which never happened.

As things remained peaceful, gradually white settlers came in small groups to take advantage of the free homestead land. While the husband was away breaking sod, the pioneer woman was left alone with her two babies. Noiselessly a moccasined Indian came unannounced into her cabin home, both hands were bloody and a blood stained knife was in his hand.

The man may have spoken to her but she never heard it, screaming she snatched up her two babes and ran to the safety of a neighboring cabin. The Indian did not follow, all he wanted was a bucket of water to cleanse the deer carcass he had slaughtered and dressed not far from the cabin.

The near hysterical woman alerted all the neighbors of the impending dangers. As a result, all gathered at one place where men held an all night vigil with muskets loaded. When no Indians with murderous intent appeared by mid-afternoon of the following day, the men ventured to take a look at the cabin where the menacing Indian had appeared. All was found in order, the water bucket was filled with fresh water from the spring and a quarter of the venison was on the kitchen table.

The Indian population in 1868 numbered approximately 6,000 members located principally on reservations. Dr. A. Branard, surgeon of the Chippewas, gave this account, "Convenient houses were built at Leech Lake in 1867 for the government employees. There were three stores, a saw and grist mill, a school and a clergyman.

"There is at Red Lake a government station, trading post, a deserted mission and two stores doing an annual business of $20,000. They have a saw and a grist mill, a physician, a miller, blacksmith and one farmer. The religious missions may be seen at Gull Lake, Winnebigoshish and Cass Lake. The principle agency and headquarters is at White Earth, Becker County, in the new reservation. $75,000 are paid annually to the 4,200 Indians on this reservation. The payments come usually in September and October.

"The most important institution of the Chippewa Tribe is the Grand Medicine, a religious society in which the traditions of the tribe are preserved and perpetuated. The society has several degrees, the highest of which is known as the 'Big Medicine Man'. This high honor is attained by few. An Indian aspiring to the honors of this ancient institution need only apply to the Grand Masters of the Order. However, to be accepted the applicant must be prepared and qualified for this honor. Should he be accepted, a suitable beast is prepared after which he is taken into the forest by the Great Medicine Man and there instructed into the properties of medicinal roots, herbs and ways of the legerdemain.

"Courtships and marriage were quite simple and not unlike the white man's in the early days. Intermarriage in families was strictly forbidden. A young brave seeking a wife goes to the lodge of his beloved. If he is an acceptable suitor in the eyes of the parents, then he may share the maiden's couch during the night. Should he remain there till morning, it is regarded as a marriage. Gifts are presented to the parents of the bride whereupon she follows the groom into his wigwam as she has become his wife.

"The life of the Chippewa woman was one of continuous toil, no different than that of her white sister. In the spring she mushes through the melting snow with her papoose upon her back and a sap bucket in either hand to the sugar bush. The buckets have been made by her out of birch bark as part of her household duties. After the sap has been boiled into that most delicious syrup, she pours it into fancy created containers made by her called 'muks kuks'. These are also made out of the bark of the birch tree and ornamented.

"After this job is completed the family moves to the fishing grounds where large supplies of fish are caught by the men and cleaned, prepared and dried by his wife.

"In June the birch bark trees yield their bark for canoes as well as for all other household purposes. Curing and preparing the bark is all her work too. She must also plant corn and potatoes. During the summer months she is occupied with the gathering of roots, wild fruits and herbs, all of which must be dried and preserved in likely spots in the earth.

"September brings the harvest of wild rice with all its duties. During the winter her husband attends to his trap lines and hunting, dutifully she follows to care for the furs, hides and the carcass for food.

"The Indian woman's spare time is devoted

to making moccasins, jackets and all the family's garments as well as beaded and painted ornaments. Occasionally she indulges, along with her neighbors, in games of amusement. The work of her nimble hands are in harmony with her spirit. Generations live together in peace and harmony; the younger women doing the heavy work while the Nocomis (grandmother) instructs the young."

The Indian women taught the white settlers how to survive in this wilderness to which they had chosen to come. She taught them how to prepare the flesh of the wild animals to make it palatable. She taught them how to select the edible roots, herbs and berries and how to prepare them for food and medicine.

The Creed of the Indian is to share and not to own. To their belief, nothing was created for one individual alone but for all mankind and for posterity.

CHAPTER XVII

Life On The Frontier

The Civil War was over as well as the racial clash of 1862. Both of these events had left serious after effects and scars upon our young state which were not taken into consideration by our state officials in planning ahead. In looking back it is not difficult to see that our young state was not prepared for so fast a pace.

Minnesota was not ripe for the advances the building of the Great Northern Railway placed upon the state. Seemingly, our governor was concerned but promoters from within as well as from the growing industrial eastern states and the ease with which the financing was secured in anticipation of rich gains took priority. That disaster struck so soon is what might have been expected.

Fortunately our state had protected our banking system through wisdom and foresight. By the end of the Civil War in 1866, Minnesota had fifteen national banks in operation. By then Congress had imposed a 10% tax upon all state banks, therefore, all had surrendered their privileges. Instantly most of the banks in Minnesota had the backing of the U.S. Government. "Greenbacks" had become depreciated and were accepted only at discount if at all.

State debt and taxes as taken from the governor's message of 1869: "The recognized debt of the state is $300,000, of which $100,000 is a loan for war purposes and $200,000 for charitable institution buildings. Taxes levied for general revenue is three mills, and for the sinking fund one mill each. This levy would amount to

$375,000. County taxes vary from 1% to 2%. School tax is two mills."

The Homestead Act of 1862 gave 160 acres free of cost to actual settlers who would reside on the land five years whether foreign or native, male or female, over twenty-one years of age or minors who had served fourteen days in the navy or army. Foreigners must declare their intention to become citizens.

A decision of the General Land Office in 1867 declared that unmarried women, whether heads of families or not, may pre-empt 160 acres of land if they are in good faith and will reside upon it.

The same law provided that eligible persons could claim 160 acres under the pre-emption law by making reasonable improvements upon the land such as building a cabin, or breaking a tract of sod, or land clearing. This would grant them prior rights to buy at $1.25 per acre over and above all others whenever the land came onto the market. As this sometimes did not occur for years, settlers may have lived on the land and made considerable improvements. When finally they were called upon to pay for the land, they would find that it had increased in price many fold.

Land offices that went into effect after the Homestead Act were at:

Douglas County
Alexandria
Register: L.K. Aaker
Receiver: J.W. VanDyke

Meeker County
Greenleaf
Register: L.M. Waldron
Receiver: J.C. Bradon

Nicolett County
St. Peter
Register: Tilson Tibbetts
Reciever: J.C. Rudolph

Jackson County

Jackson

Register: J.B. Wakefield

Receiver: E.P. Freeman

Stearns County

St. Cloud

Register: C.A. Gilman

Receiver: R.H.C. Burbank

Chisago County

Taylors Falls

Register: J.P. Owens

Receiver: R.L.K. Stannard

St. Louis County

Duluth

Address Register at Duluth

All of the above areas still had thousands of free homesteads for settlers waiting as of November, 1869.

In almost every county in the state wild

lands owned by speculators could be purchased for from $5.00 to $10.00 per acre, part cash and credit for up to five years; however, interest was 7% on deferred payments. Railroad lands within six miles of any railroad could be had for from $5.00 to $10.00 with only a small down payment and up to ten years to pay. School lands sold for $5.00 to $8.00 with 15% cash and credit up to twenty years.

State Laws, Exemptions, Redemptions, Rights For Women

A homestead of eighty acres and improvements in the country, or one house and lot in town without regard to value was exempt from execution. Also exempt were $500 in furniture, all wearing apparel, beds, bedding, stoves, utensils. A wagon, cart, dray, two plows, sleigh and other farming implements not exceeding $300 were exempt. Also, three cows, ten swine, one yoke of oxen, one horse or span of horses or mules, twenty sheep, and twelve months provisions for family and stock.

Exemptions were allowed for a mechanic's

tools, $400 stock in trade and the library of a professional man PROVIDED that none of this property is exempt from execution on a suit for the purchase money of same, or from mechanic's liens for labor or materials in making or repairing the same.

Real estate sold under execution or mortgage may be redeemed in twelve months by paying the debt at 7%.

Soon after the first frontier woman set foot upon her wilderness home she had her rights protected by the law reading as follows. "Married women are entitled to as full rights of property as if single. Both their property before and after marriage and the avails of her industry or business are free from the control of her husbands' or liability of his debts. They may contract and be contracted with as single women, except in relation to real estate. This was by act of March 1869."

Many of the women exercised this right by filing on land, or often on pre-emption claims. It was not unusual for a widow with a family of children to be among a group coming in caravans of covered wagons to locate on a wilderness claim. They were hoping to produce food and shelter in an environment where the family could remain together with the full realization of the hardships and discomforts. But, the dangers they were to find could not be anticipated by any of these hardy people.

Public Libraries, Telegraphy and Stages

By the year of 1869 our State Library and Historical Society located at St. Paul had 3,100 volumes, 5,200 pamphlets, 233 maps, a number of portraits, engravings, bound newspapers and a fine cabinet of Indian artifacts.

Telegraphic connections with all points east and south existed in all the Mississippi River towns, with Stillwater, with all towns on the railroad lines, as well as with Duluth and Lake Superior.

Stages ran as far west as Fort Abercrombie on the Red River and Jackson County, and as far north as Fort Ripley and Duluth connecting with all the railroads.

In 1858 when Minnesota Territory was accepted into the Union, the government surveyed and laid out a road from St. Cloud to Fort Abercrombie. Soon settlers began to move into all areas so that by June 1859 the J. C. & Company stages began to operate. As far northwest as Douglas County a stage house was opened at Chippewa, which also had a post office. This name was later changed to Brandon. This stage carried the mail from St. Cloud to Fort Abercrombie.

CHAPTER XVIII

Women's Rights On The Frontier

The Seven Demerling Sisters

Among the many hundreds of settlers who came to Minnesota in an ox drawn caravan of covered wagons, or in very rare cases by a span of horses, after the passing of the Homestead Act in 1867, was a caravan of a dozen families from Ohio.

Their destination was the paradise

described by promoters as the "Big Woods", sixty miles north of St. Paul. Into this wilderness no white woman had ever trod and only a few white men. In general they were second generation Americans. Some men had participated in the Civil War, the after effects of which had impoverished them to the extent that they were compelled to seek an independent way of life for themselves and their dependants.

The Demerlings were in this caravan. Five sisters of that large family came, their ages were from fourteen to twenty-three. Olivia, twenty-three, and Rosalie anticipated ownership of their claims. The parents, with two younger girls, remained in Ohio because the father had not recovered from the wounds suffered in the war and the mother was a bedridden invalid. Seventeen year old twins, Maggie and Lucy, remained to care for their parents and to acquire a better education which would fit them for teaching positions in Minnesota.

The three youngest Demerlings, Veronica sixteen, Ruby fifteen and fourteen year old Kari, found the trip most exciting wishing it would never end. After many days of slow, tedious travel it finally did end, having now arrived at St. Paul. Their future home was still sixty miles to the north, St. Paul being their last stop before entering into the unknown wilderness.

It was in the early days of April and already the going was becoming heavier with each passing mile, but all they saw was Minnesota bursting into all its springtime glories so full of promises awaiting the strangers.

In St. Paul they removed the harnesses from their horses and the heavy wooden yokes of their oxen for rest, feed and water. Now the head of each wagon went forth into the city to conduct their legal affairs at the State House. Olivia and Rosalie Demerling were among those who filed for a homestead of eighty acres each. After this another day was spent in making needed purchases, and money as well as wagon space was limited. Although the needs were many, care was taken that duplicate purchases were avoided. By sharing tools, help, equipment and advice they would all be better off.

The five Demerlings departed somewhat from this rule by making purchases of yards and yards of sturdy brightly colored calicoes along with good solid leather boots for each. Their other purchases consisted of two cows, a dozen hens and feed, along with such staples as salt, flour, matches and leavening agents for baking. All the seeds were carried all the way from Ohio.

The wagons were loaded to capacity and the teams found traveling heavy through the early spring thaw, which made it necessary for all the able bodied to walk behind their wagons the greater part of the sixty mile trip. It took most of the week, but their morale remained high.

An officer on horseback accompanied the caravan and remained with them until all knew the extent of their holdings. The Demerlings selected a grassy knoll near a fine free flowing fresh water spring. Their homesteads joined as close to the others as possible. The sisters were fully aware of their incompetence as far as agriculture was concerned; their experience consisted of having planted the family's backyard gardens in their former home of Ohio.

"It's all ours," said Olivia softly. "Let us thank our dear Lord and ask His blessings upon this great undertaking. We will continue to live much as we have been living for the past weeks. We will use the great outdoors for our housekeeping and sleep inside our wagons until all the other neighbors have finished their new homes. We are all adults and can wait while families with children need the shelter and security of a cabin now." In the year of 1867 women and young girls all wore long sweeping skirts with flounces and ruffles at the hemlines. Often they were so long that they required binding at the edges to absorb the wear of dragging in the dirt and grit. Not even in her home did a lady depart from this rule.

The Demerlings may very well have been the first, not only to design, but also to wear pantsuits. It was of necessity because they were about to spend most of their time doing outdoor men's work. Out of the varicolored calico they made neat fitting pants, shirts and jackets. To satisfy their feminine egos, they applied a ruffle here and a bit of hand embroidery there but, even so, they did not wear these garments with pride.

Nor did these young ladies feel proud in laying the ax to the healthy young timber to make way for the plow and logs for their cabin. The first task for all the settlers was to clear a parcel of land to get their seeds planted. They had been told that frost comes early in Minnesota, as early as September first.

By the time the Demerlings had their tract cleared and planted they had acquired sufficient experience to continue on their own and even to help their neighbors. Blistered hands had hardened into calluses and sunburned, freckled noses were accepted, if not appreciated. After the planting the need was for fences and enclosures for their cows. Felling the trees, removing the bark and building their own rail fences became an outline for their cabins and future home.

The labor was eased as they could now envision a home with their beloved family together again. The days were long and rest periods short, but Sundays were the day of rest for the young colony of settlers. It was the day all looked forward to.

Wearing the pretty dresses they had brought with them, the sisters joined their friends and neighbors in a clearing under the spreading branches of an ancient oak tree for a few hours of worship to Him from whom they expected so much. It was also a day of rest, relaxation and for the young, who never tire on a day of fun and recreation. After their period of worship, they shared in a hearty lunch consisting of the carefully stored delicacies they may have brought from Ohio and later on the samplings of the fresh berries ripening in the summer sun. The adults now held their weekly meeting and discussions relating their triumphs and the many disappointments and failures. They were together and shared alike in whatever they had, good or bad.

The glorious days passed all to soon and the early tinges of autumn brought the settlers to understand that indeed the seasons are short in Minnesota. The days shortened, but the working hours remained the same because the cabins must be soon in shape for winter use, barns had to be erected for the livestock and feed provided for the long months ahead. The sisters helped wherever they were needed, but they were not considered equal to any of them in any of the tasks confronting them.

Finally the happy day arrived when all the neighbors came with all the tools and equipment they had to erect the Demerling home.

This, however, was not just another cabin but a two story home with an annex. "We have a large family," said Olivia thoughtfully. "There are nine of us. Not only must there be room for all us nine adults, but there must be comfort for our invalid mother and our ailing father."

Men and women helped eagerly and gladly until the last birch shingle was in place. With pride it was called MANSION. It was generally accepted that the best was none too good to bring the ailing parents of the Demerling sisters to. While all the cabins had but a dirt floor for the first winter, the Demerlings brought in dry marsh grass which they spread evenly and tamped down to a depth of six inches. Over this they stretched a rug they had made out of bear hides to cover the entire floor. The small windows had ruffled curtains arranged as a frame so as not to interfere with any sunlight from entering in. It was truly the first mansion in Minnesota's wilderness, named the "Big Woods".

Within the intervening time the Pacific Railroad had extended a branch called Darsel's Station to within twenty miles from the settlement of these twelve homesteaders in the "Big Woods". Although it ran only on alternate days and at irregular times, it was never-the-less a great boon to the settlers who could now travel by train to St. Paul to conduct their business.

Now that the house was ready for occupancy, the Demerlings decided that Rosalie should travel to Ohio to bring their parents back to Minnesota along with their twin sisters without further delay. Rosalie would take the train from Darsel's Station as soon as a group of neighbors could be organized to make the trip.

Three teams were soon readied to make the two day round trip. Those who had produce to ship to St. Paul sent it along too. They traveled in their covered wagons as it would be an overnight stay to rest and feed the horses. Letters were written to friends and families back in Ohio to be mailed while some were entrusted to Rosalie to be delivered personally. The day of departure was one of excitement and eager anticipation as well as of concern for the safe return of the travelers.

When Rosalie, after many days of weary travel, arrived at her former home in Ohio she was overwhelmed with family and friends wishing to hear news from their loved ones from whom they had not heard since the caravan arrived in St. Paul in April. They loaded her with letters and parcels to take back with her.

Rosalie found her family packed and happily awaiting her arrival. Although sad to leave their home and life-long friends, the elder Demerlings were lonely for their five daughters and were eager to leave at once in anticipation of being a united family again.

The trip was slow and tedious for the ailing Demerlings. When they finally arrived at Darsel's Station, five wagons were patiently waiting. Kari and Ruby had come in the Demerlings covered wagon and it was soon made comfortable with the addition of pillows and feather beds which the elder Demerlings had brought from Ohio. The other wagons were loaded with the family's furnishings and supplies for over winter as well as parcels for the other settlers with gifts from their families.

The arrival of the four Demerlings changed the community overnight. The twins, Maggie and Lucy, had brought copies of McGuffy's Readers, slates, pencils and other school supplies for the settlement's first school. The family's most prized possession was also packed along with the feather beds. The mother, being a musician, had taught all her daughters to play this fine instrument..., it was a pianoforte.

As the neighbors came calling, they learned that Maggie and Lucy, now eighteen, were qualified to teach the youngsters of the new community. As there was no building available, the Demerlings used their newly finished annex for classes as there were now ten youngsters of school age. Not only did the youngsters come, but the teenagers who brought them also attended classes.

The approach of colder weather halted the outdoor Sunday worship hour and weekly meeting. As this was deeply felt by all, it was only natural that the Demerling annex would have to serve the purpose until a building could be erected. Each Sunday the neighbors gathered there for prayer, worship, Bible reading and singing to the soft music of the pianoforte played by their oldest member, the mother that was housebound and happy to have them there. After a hearty pot luck lunch consisting chiefly of a variety of stews made with the meat from the forest, their own vegetables and hot corn bread, they returned to their own cabins refreshed in body and mind and eager for the coming week.

The Demerling sisters were second generation Americans and, therefore, adapted to the hardships, trials, privations and loneliness of the frontier. During the following year a cabin was erected on Rosalie's claim with the help of all the neighbors. It was an oversized building so that it could be used as a school as well as for a house of worship or for meetings.

Within three years the girls had half of their land cleared and in production and their buildings and fences kept in repair. Their yards and gardens were an inspiration for the community. After the first log school was built on school land, the twin sisters, Maggie and Lucy, continued to alternate in teaching the Three R's as well as religion to the ever-increasing younger population. Others assisted their neighbors by spinning, sewing, nursing, or with their letter writing and business affairs.

END

The story of the Demerlings is fiction based upon statistical records. The location and time is true, as well as the several sisters homesteading in the "Big Woods". It is also true that they brought their ailing parents there. Although the mother never regained her health, the father did and could assist in light work and give advice.

CHAPTER XVIV

A 1869 Check List
of the Cost Of Living

Beef by the quarter $.07-$.O8, steaks and roasts $.15-$.20; pork $.08-1/2-$.10, steaks $.18-$.20; mutton $.15-$.20; venison in quantity $.08; steaks; $.18; chicken $.12-1/2-$.l5; turkey $.15-$.18; fish $.05 - $.15.

Lard $.20-$.25; flour $5.00 per barrel; meal $.04; buckwheat flour $1.50 per sack (no weight given); butter $.25-$.30; cheese $.20; eggs $.35 per dozen; potatoes $1.00 per bushel;

rutabagas $.35 per bushel; onions $.75; beans $.45 per bushel; cranberries $1.75 per bushel; sugar $.14 - $.16 per pound; coffee $.22 - $.28 per pound; tea $.90 - $1.80 per pound.

Wood $6.00 - $7.50 per cord; rent $3.00 - $15.00 per month for cottages, houses $15.00 - $50.00 per month; board $1.00-$3.00 per day, or $4.00-$6.00 per week.

Dry goods — calicoes $.08 - $.12-1/2 per yard; brown sheetings $.12-1/2 - $.16; bleached cotton $.13 - $.18; brown shirtings $.10 -$.14; domestic gingham $.14 - $.17 per yard; blankets wool $3.50 - $9.00 per pair; grey blankets $.50 per pound.

Cost of building four to five rooms $600 - $800; houses of eight to ten rooms $1,000 - $3,500, according to style and size; lumber $15.00 per M; fencing $17.00; shingles $3.00 - $4.50; dimensions $17.00; plastering $.30 per yard; two coats painting $.18 - $.24 per yard; nails $.05 - $.07 per pound; masonry $2.00 - $3.50 per perch.

To aid men of limited means it was hopeful that an association could be organized in St. Paul which would spread all over the state and enable its members to build homes by paying annually from eight to ten years; about the same as paying rent and at about the same amount.

Wages -- carpenter $2.00 - $3.00 per day; masons $3.50 -$4.50 per day; painters $2.00 - $3.00 per day; laborers $1.50 - $2.00 per day. Laborers by the month $20.00 - $30.00 on farms, $35.00 - $60.00 on boats. Servants $8.00 per month, clerks $5.00 - $18.00 per month, teachers $300 - $1,500 annually.

CHAPTER XX

Minnesota's Valiant Women

The pioneers ventured into Minnesota to settle upon land of which they knew so very little, hoping to derive sustenance and independence for themselves and their children. They were fully aware that this would come about only through their own hard earned efforts. They came well endowed with energy and determination, both of which they applied endlessly because they had so little else.

Whether there was a harvest or not, it was entirely up to the wife and mother to provide food for her family. Even the best harvest provided only the raw materials. It was up to our pioneering women to turn the precious God given grains, fruits, vegetables, herbs and wild meat into palatable meals. This required not only considerable brawn, but intelligent manipulation unlike that of any cook today.

This cook of yesteryear didn't even have a stove with an oven in which to bake her bread. If she was very fortunate, she had an oven built into one side of the cabin's fireplace, which was her sole heating unit for all her cooking, preserving or fat rendering.

The immigrating families stocked their wagons at the last shopping point with staple foods, of which flour was perhaps the most cherished item. Flour of that period was stone ground or crushed and retained all its nutritive qualities, one of which was the grain germ. Therefore, the flour did not keep for lengthy periods in warm weather and space was also limited. In some instances this precious commodity was lost in crossing some of the many unbridged streams. In such unfortunate cases, the family arrived at their new homesite in the wilderness with a bare cupboard.

With no house ready to move into, the wagon remained as their home until a cabin could be erected. A crude outdoor fireplace was hurriedly constructed of available clay and stone on which to cook what food they could forage from the lakes and forest. In spite of this, our pioneering grandmothers baked bread for their families. Here is how this writer's grandmother performed the impossible!

Freder'ica met and married her husband Fredelyn Joos in New York, both being immigrants, and from there they moved to Pennsylvania. After some years and three children later this couple, along with some of their friends, decided to move west to the new territory of Minnesota. Exact dates are unknown as all except their lives was lost later on during the racial clash of 1862.

Fredelyn was a husky young Alsatian

Frenchman and his tiny blue-eyed wife came from the Swabian Mountains of Germany. She came endowed with natural stamina and intelligence. At the time the couple planned this long, dangerous move into the unknown wilderness of Minnesota, Freder'ica found herself pregnant with her fourth child. She kept this as her secret from the members of their group as well as from her husband.

The group traveled by train to Prairie du Chien, which was the railroad terminal. Here they moved into hotels and began the tedious task of shopping for wagons, oxen, cows, chickens, possibly a few pigs, feed, seeds, implements and food. The spring rains turned the environment into a quagmire of mud so that any progress was slow, expensive and tedious.

By this time Freder'ica's secret was common gossip among their group members and also a matter of great concern, especially to her husband. At great length it was decided that the Joos family must remain in Prairie du Chien while the others must move on to their destination.

In due time Freder'ica's fourth child, a son, was born. Fourscore later his son, now grown to full manhood, was to become my father.

As soon as possible the family started on their journey westward. It was now mid-September and the springtime mud had dried, so the trip was made in an endless cloud of dust created by the many wagons and the trodding of cattle.

After about six weeks they arrived at their new destination with a new son, a cow with a new calf, but no flour. The village of Prairie du Chien had no flour, as wheat had not been brought in yet from the new crop. The friends who had gone ahead in spring had broken an acreage which had been planted and was now being harvested. A scanty supply to be sure, but they shared it with the Joos family. Since there was no garden either, the family gathered nuts, herbs, roots and later cranberries in great quantities, all of which were diligently dried and stored for the long winter months ahead.

The neighbors were most helpful in getting

the cabin ready and comfortable for Freder'ica, her son and the family, but still there was no flour in the new settlement. Freder'ica baked bannocks for her family by soaking the newly harvested wheat in warm water and squeezing them between the palms of her strong, firm hands. She soon had the gluttony pulp severed from its skins; as these were lighter they easily floated upon the water and could be skimmed off. After this she carefully drained all the water away leaving only her "batter". To this she added a pinch of salt and a pinch of her most precious sour dough, which she managed to bring from their former home in Pennsylvania. She also had an egg to add from her hens in the crate beneath the wagon.

By the time Freder'ica had all this prepared, the soapstone on the shelf of the outdoor fireplace was hot. She carefully portioned the batter into bakes leaving them to bake until they had risen and were done on the underside, then she deftly flipped them over to bake until done. The resulting bannocks were delicious as well as nutritious. They resembled knackebrod and could be stored for future use. The residue of the wheat was fed to the cow.

Later in the season, after the ground had frozen and before the winter's snow and storms came, the settlers took their wheat to St. Paul, which was the nearest grist mill, to have their winter supply of wheat stone ground. This was a two day trip and was never undertaken by one man and wagon alone. When at long last the first stone ground flour arrived at the cabin, Freder'ica lost no time in baking real loaves of good bread again.

Wild hops grew in abundance. Freder'ica and the children gathered quantities of the delicate blossoms, dried and had them stored in a cloth bag to be used by the immigrant family for bread leavening or medicinal purposes.

To start the fragile yeast cells into life, a sweetening agent is quite necessary. Costly sugar was not found in the cupboards on the frontier, but watermelons were bursting with nature's very own sweetened juice. Freder'ica, along with her neighbors, carefully removed all the tender flesh of the melons and then crushed the pulp into mush, after which the juice was easily extracted. This was carefully strained through cloth and slowly boiled into syrup. It was then canned in bottle shaped jars where it was made to last until spring would bring the maple sugar harvest.

To make her bread dough, Freder'ica put a handful of the dried hops to soak in warm water overnight, after which it was strained into a tall crock. Later the water was strained off a pot of peeled, boiled potatoes and, when cooled, it was added, along with a tablespoonful of the condensed melon juice, to the hop tea. It was then set uncovered in the ever warm chimney corner.

Before retiring for the night Freder'ica poured her dough starter into a large crock leaving about a pint in the container, which she covered and stored in the pit. (The pit was a hollowed out cavity beneath the floor of the cabin with a trap door. It was used to store root vegetables to keep them from freezing.) Flour was stirred into the dough starter. The crock was then covered with a cloth and replaced in the warm chimney corner.

By morning Freder'ica found the contents of the crock bubbling and threatening to overflow unless she would stir it down at once and get her bread mixed. Often she took a cup of this yeasty batter to make a hearty batch of buckwheat cakes for breakfast, or perhaps a molasses cake, or fried cakes (doughnuts). Such treats were to come much later after the family had their own maple sugar and syrup.

Early in the day Freder'ica set about to mix her bread dough for a batch of twelve to fourteen loaves. Fredelyn had carved her a bread mixer out of the round of log of the black walnut, selecting the part right above the root. This was carefully carved and smoothed until it had the smoothness of a china bowl. It was then scrubbed, dried and polished. A concave cover to fit was also made and this fine receptacle was used only for the kneading and rising of bread dough.

Bake day was a family affair, but it came only on alternate weeks. Early on bake day Fredelyn kindled a fire in the outdoor clay oven and kept adding until the time was close to where the loaves were ready to be baked. Meanwhile Freder'ica scrubbed the wide pine boards of her kitchen table and, given time to dry, she then sprinkled cornmeal over the surface of the table.

After the dough had risen in volume sufficiently to be shaped into loaves, she dumped the dough onto her prepared table, divided it into twelve to fourteen parts, formed each into a long narrow loaf and placed each upon the hand-wrought metal pan which was made to fit the oven. The pan had previously been sprinkled lightly with cornmeal, no shortening or fat was used in this bread. Depending upon the temperature in the cabin, within two hours the loaves were ready to be baked. If the rising period was prolonged due to too low a temperature, the bread became sour, which made it less palatable but never useless.

Meanwhile Fredelyn had removed all the embers and ashes from the oven. He brought in a bucket of clay from a nearby likely spot and mixed it with water to form a smooth spreading consistency. When all was in readiness Fredelyn carefully carried the large pan with its precious load out to the waiting oven, replaced the door and sealed it with the moist clay. It was given no further attention.

The following morning the oven was opened and the crispy brown loaves of total whole wheat bread were brought into the kitchen. Can one possibly imagine what a feast the family had that morning? Freder'ica did not slice her loaf on a bread board. She took the long crusty loaf underneath her arm and deftly sliced thick slices for each member that sat around the pineboard table on crude log benches.

First of all, grace and thanks was given to God from whom all this came. The long prayers had given the bowls of mush a bit of time to cool. After prayers the bread was broken into the bowl of mush, made usually of cornmeal, and milk was poured over it in generous quantities. Such were the breakfasts in nearly every frontier home.

CHAPTER XXI

A Potpourri Of Early Minnesota Bread
Recipes, And Others

It was a long time until flour and meal could be bought bagged in stores. In most cases the grain producer took his grain to the mill where he had it crushed or stone ground. It was not sifted or separated, but used whole. As soon as flour mills came into the state, the stone ground product was separated into flour, middlings and bran, which is the outer shell of the wheat. The miller received a certain percent of this product for his labor which he could sell to those who did not produce grain. It came in barrels or the buyer brought his own cloth bag along.

The flour was not white but a rich creamy color and felt somewhat moist. It still contained the live wheat germ and, therefore, did not keep well in warm weather. The flour always required several siftings to remove any fragments of stone. The cook also knew that the sifting would result in a lighter loaf.

Later, when wood burning kitchen stoves came into use, pans and pots were usually given as an extra bonus. The manufacturers knew that the stove without the pots and pans would be useless, as kitchen utensils of the fireplace period could not be used with the new stoves with ovens.

The new pots and pans now came with the insides enameled and the bottoms flat to fit the lids of the new stoves. The bread pans came in various sizes, but all were made of metal called japanned steel. They were medium light weight, very durable, practically indestructible and similar to the teflon of today. These pans required no greasing. All that was required was to wipe them with a damp cloth and dry with a soft cloth until they gleamed. My mother kept each pan in its own brown paper bag. As I recall, she had a separate pan for every use.

Ovens in wood burning stoves produce a gentle heat compared to the intense heat of gas or electricity. This may have been the reasons that these pans gave such excellent results.

Recipe For Brown Bread
3 cups sour milk
1 tablespoon salt
½ cup sugar
2 tablespoons soda
3 tablespoons molasses
1 cup flour
4 cups whole wheat flour

Dissolve soda in sour milk, add molasses. Combine all dry ingredients. Add the milk mixture, beat well and divide into two loaf pans. Allow to stand 45 minutes. Bake in slow oven until done, about 45 minutes.

Witches Brew Bread

Combine two quarts potatoe water, two boiled mashed potatoes and ½ cup sugar. After this is lukewarm, crumble two dry yeast cakes into it. Set aside uncovered where the temperature remains the same for twelve hours. After this time stir the mixture well, cover and set into a cool, dark place -- the cellar was used, but the refrigerator will do nicely. The following morning it is again stirred and 1/2 quart taken out, which is set into a cool place to be used for the next baking. The remainder was used to mix a large batch of bread. A quart or even two of warm, never hot, water was added as well as 1/4 cup of sugar and salt to taste (about two tablespoons full). Flour was added to make a medium batter, after which it was well beaten. This was called 'the sponge' and was allowed to raise until it was bubbly and light. It was then turned into the bread mixer where flour was added until it was of kneading consistency. Thorough kneading was important as this brought out the gluten of the wheat and gave the finished loaf its fine texture, volume and flavor. The dough was punched down once and left to rise a second time. When it was ready to form into loaves, a pan of biscuits was made, or cinnamon rolls, for the families coffee break in the afternoon.

My Mother's Bread Recipe With Variations

Preparations began at noon for baking the following day. The potatoe water from the pot of boiled potatoes mother cooked for our noontime dinner was drained into a suitable crock. 1/4 cup of sugar was stirred into it and then it was left in a warm place. In the evening she soaked a yeast cake in lukewarm water and added it to the potatoe water. If it was not lukewarm anymore, it was reheated. She mixed flour into this until she had a soft batter. Uncovered it was set into a warm spot and left overnight.

Yeast cakes came six to a pack and they were dry and compressed having been made of cornmeal, rye flour and yeast. They required no refrigeration and kept for as long as six months, Freezing destroyed the tender yeast cell. One cake of this leavened a batch of ten to twelve large loaves. Although no one knew why, but every

179

cook knew that the bread gets better when the yeast or sponge is left uncovered at room temperature. Today we know that yeast cells float unseen in the air, particularly in warm kitchens where fresh produce is usually found. These cells contribute to the palatability of the bread.

The morning of mother's bake day found her early tending to her sponge, which was now a lively, bubbling mass. Quite often she would give me the pleasant task of sifting and resifting five sifters of flour into her heavy metal bread mixing bowl. Pushing the flour aside she poured the sponge into the cavity left there, usually she added a dipper or two of lukewarm water. Great care was taken that it was never too warm or too cool as the yeast cell is a tiny one cell plant easily destroyed.

With her long handled wooden spoon she deftly gathered the flour into the sponge until she could no longer wield it. Then she went in with both hands adding handfuls of flour and kneading until she had a non-sticky compact ball and the sides of the pan were clean and free of flour or dough. Mother never used shortening in her dough or on the loaves. After the compact ball was formed, it was then covered with the concave cover which fit securely into the groove on the pan made for this purpose.

After about two hours it was ready to punch down and given another hour to rise. Although it had not doubled in volume, she considered it time to form into loaves. As mother formed her bread loaves she sprinkled cornmeal on the bread board where she rolled the dough into forms. She also sprinkled cornmeal into the bottoms of the bread pans. The loaves came out a delicious crispy golden brown with hard crusts which we enjoyed so very much.

The same method was used to bake a variety of breads such as graham, whole wheat, oatmeal or rye bread. The basic recipe for coffee cakes, raised doughnuts, buns, biscuits and so on was as follows: One quart fresh milk from the morning milking, scalded and cooled; two eggs beaten until they are lemon colored; two cups sugar and one cup butter, creamed; one tablespoon salt, one-quarter teaspoon grated nutmeg or maize; one yeast cake dissolved in a little lukewarm water to which a pinch of sugar has been added. Mix all together and add flour until it is of a soft, yet non-sticky consistency.

Out of this recipe a large variety of delicious treats were made. For coffee cakes and buns, raisins and currents were added. These fruits came in bulk in wooden crates. It was necessary to hand pick them to remove seeds as well as dried particles of the plant. Many rinsings removed all this after which they were dried on a towel.

Raisins were fat and plump, about the size of a nickel, but their seeds were still inside and had to be removed by hand. However, every well equipped kitchen had a raisin seeder, a nutmeg grater and a hand mill to grind pepper, allspice, cinnamon sticks, as well as coffee.

Aunt Mary's Gräphen

Aunt Mary was an immigrant from Bavaria and an excellent cook. Her strudel and gräphen were delicacies not easily forgotten. They resembled raised doughnuts but were infinitely lighter and crunchier. Her recipe called for two eggs beaten light and fluffy, one-half cup butter and one cup sugar creamed, a quart of scalded and cooled milk combined with the creamed sugar and eggs, and one teaspoon salt was added. She soaked a cake of dry yeast in lukewarm water to which a teaspoon of sugar was added. After this was dissolved, she combined all the ingredients and added flour to make a light batter. It was then set aside into a spot to "work" for perhaps thirty minutes.

Now she gave her bubbling batter a few good turns with her long handled wooden spoon and added thrice sifted flour until it could no longer be mixed by spoon. It was then at the kneading stage so she continued to sift flour lightly and knead the dough until it formed a non-sticky ball. She rubbed melted butter over it, covered the bowl and set it aside to rise. This took two hours.

Aunt Mary's white enamel lined cast iron kettle was already on her wood burning kitchen stove heating the pure leaf lard in which she baked her gräphen. The dough having risen to the desired lightness and with the lard at just the right temperature, she would snip off a walnut sized lump of the dough and nimbly manipulate it into a round form that was tissue paper thin in the center with a slight build-up around the edges. This circle was gently, but ever so quickly, dropped into the hot lard. Within a moment it came up golden brown with the center a creamy white morsel so fragile it required careful handling so as not to break it. It was placed upon a wire rack to cool slightly after which each was sprinkled with a mixture of sugar and cinnamon or nutmeg.

Grandmother's Spicy Molasses Cake

1 cup butter and lard or tallow mixed and
melted
2 eggs beaten until lemon colored
1 cup black strap molasses or sorghum
2 cups sour or buttermilk
1 teaspoon salertus (soda)
1 teaspoon cream of tartar, 1/2 teaspoon
salt

1 cup raisins with seeds removed

1 teaspoon ginger, sprinkle of allspice, dash of cardamom or cinnamon or grating of nutmeg.

Sifted flour to make a medium batter.

Combine all dry ingredients and raisins, blend in the melted fat, milk and, lastly, the eggs. Bake in a large pan at medium heat for 45-60 minutes. The only icing that was used was a meringue made of the beaten white of an egg or two and a spoonful of sugar. It was then set into a hot oven to cook quickly.

Indian Bread

To three cups flour add two teaspoons salt, one teaspoon soda dissolved in water, and cold water to make a dough firm enough to form into biscuit sized patties. Knead the dough before shaping and allow a short period of rising. Then pinch small portions off and pull it into a thin cake and bake in hot bear's lard. Turn once and serve hot with honey or sorghum.

Crackling Bread

To two cups cornmeal take one-half cup flour, salt to taste, one cup cracklings, two eggs and one teaspoon salertus (soda) dissolved in one cup buttermilk. Mix all together and bake in a large shallow pan about 30 minutes or until the top is crisp and golden brown. Cracklings are the crisp bits left over after rendering lard. Should be used when fresh only.

Pasties

Vegetable-meat mix: two cups raw chopped meat; four large raw potatoes, sliced or diced; one raw onion, sliced or grated; cubed carrots or other vegetables may be added. Mix well and set on one side. Make a crust of three cups flour, one cup lard, salt, and cold water (about one-half cup). Roll thin in circles the size of a dinner plate. Place vegetable-meat mixture on one side, season with salt and pepper. Moisten the edge, fold over and press edges down with a fork. Bake for an hour. After ten minutes lower the heat and after forty minutes make a small slit into the top of each and add a teaspoonful of hot water to each pastie.

Frenchmen's Pork Pie

Chop three cups fresh lean pork with a large onion, add salt and pepper and cook slowly until meat is tender and the liquid is boiled down to one cup. Season to taste (cinnamon was a favorite) and thicken with a spoonful of flour dissolved in a bit of cold water. Cool. Make a medium rich pie crust for a deep round pan and pour the mix into the crust lined pan. Cover with another crust which has many slits to allow steam to escape. Bake until done and browned on top. Serve hot or cold.

Frontierman's Favorite Cranberry Pudding

Beat one egg, add one-half cup molasses, maple syrup or honey, salt, one and one-half cups flour, one-half cup cranberries, two teaspoons salertus (soda) dissolved in one-half cup hot water. Mix all ingredients and tie it into a cloth bag.

Steam two hours over hot water. Serve with a sauce made with one-half cup butter and one-half cup cream heated but not boiled.

Scotch Cake

One cup molasses, one-half honey may be used, one cup sour cream, one and one-half teaspoon salertus (soda), one and one-half cups flour or enough to make a medium batter. Beat eggs until thick, add molasses or honey and beat again. Add cream into which the salertus has been dissolved, add the flour and any spices if desired. Raisins or nuts may be added. Bake in a deep bread pan until done, 45-50 minutes at medium heat.

Fattigman Bakkels

One whole egg, two egg yolks, one tablespoon sweet cream, pinch salt, pinch of cinnamon or nutmeg, pinch sugar. Beat eggs, sugar and cream. Add flour until it has the consistency that it can be rolled out as for noodles. Roll very thin and cut in pieces 2x4 inches. Cut a slit an inch from one end and lace a corner from the side through the slit forming a bow knot. Fry in hot deep fat, drain and sprinkle with sugar and cinnamon.

Sugar was a commodity not easily found on the frontier. What was available was unrefined, crude brown sugar.

Suet Pudding

Chop equal portions of suet, raisins, apples or nuts to fill a quart measure. Add one cup molasses, one cup sweet milk, one teaspoon salertus (soda) dissolved in one-quarter cup hot water, three cups flour, pinch salt, cinnamon or other spice. Mix and tie into a cloth bag and steam for three hours.

Brent Mehl Süppe (Browned Flour Soup)

A cup of flour or more, depending upon

family size, is placed into a heavy cast iron pan, set over a low heat and stirred with a wooden spoon until the entire mass is evenly browned, being careful not to scorch it. Warm, not hot, water is added slowly while stirring and cooking is continued as for gravy. Salt to taste and add a lump of butter the size of a walnut. If it is too thick, water or milk may be added, or a bit of cream. Served with buttered bread this made a complete supper for the family.

German Brei

Brei is a soup made of milk fresh from the cow with a bit of flour and salt. The secret is in the long boiling without scorching. For this an enamel lined cast iron kettle was preferred. A gallon of milk was poured into the kettle and set over a slow wood fire. Two cups of flour and a tablespoon of salt were blended with a cup of the milk and slowly stirred into the milk in the kettle. Stirring was continued until the raw flavor had completely changed into a creamy delicacy. It was served hot or cold on hot summer evenings and with buttered bread it constituted the family's supper.

Fried Bread With Backwoods Preserves

Dip slices of very dry bread quickly into cold water, then into beaten eggs to which a pinch of salt has been added. Fry in deep hot lard until nicely browned on both sides. Serve the backwoods preserves.

Bring to a slow boil two cups molasses. Add three well beaten eggs stirring continually and boil a minute or so longer to cook the egg. Grate a bit of nutmeg into it and serve hot or cooled.

Frontier Brown Bread

For each large loaf take one and one-half cups cornmeal, pour boiling water over to scald it, let stand until blood warm. Add one quart rye flour and a good sized bowl of emptyings with a little salertus (soda) stirred in. No salt is needed. Add flour and knead as for any bread. Mold into a long loaf and set aside to rise an hour. Bake two hours.

An old dictionary defines the word emptyings as the settlings in the bottom of a beer or cider keg.

Immigrant's Bread

Since man invented fire to cook his food, bread in some form has been cooked. Prior to the advent of ovens, bread was cooked as we still cook our Boston Brown Bread or as pudding tied in bags made of leaves, animal hides or even the skin of large fish. Bread in some form was of prime importance to the human family.

The bread which the European immigrants brought along to the New World was made of barley, rye and oats, stone ground. Any wheat which was produced there was not used for bread for the peasantry; this was only for the wealthy ones and then only for grand occasions.

No leavening or salt was used in bread. The peasant kitchen in Europe had a huge trough-shaped table into which the coarse stone ground grain was poured. Mashed potatoes, cabbage, pumpkins and turnips were boiled tender, mashed and added to the grain. Sour clabbered milk was added when available. This was thoroughly mixed then left to "set" until fermentation started.

When the mash had reached the desired degree of fermentation it had become a somewhat doughy consistency. The cook, who was usually the mother, knew by the odor when her mash was "ripe". With a wooden long handled scoop she floured until she could no longer stir the dough. After this she rolled up her sleeves and kneaded until it could be formed into long narrow loaves.

The kitchen table had previously been scrubbed and dried. She sprinkled flour on the top and placed all her loaves to rest. The cook's work was now finished. From here on "her man" took over. A wife referred to her husband as "her man" and the husband referred to his wife as "his woman".

The huge outdoor clay oven was soon ready. With a long wooden spade the husband carried the long narrow heavy loaves out arranging them so that the six weeks' supply of bread could all be accommodated. The opening was then closed and carefully sealed with moist clay. After many hours, usually 30-35, the oven was opened and the bread was done. It had shrunk and was hard as rocks. It was allowed to cool thoroughly and was then loosely packed into strong cloth bags, firmly tied and hung up on rafters of their food storage house or in their kitchen.

After six weeks of aging, the bread had mellowed sufficiently so that thick slices could be cut. It was always sour and heavy, but that was the way they liked their bread. It was hearty fare and must have given them good health as these people lived long lives never knowing about dental problems, arthritis or heart failures.

However, after they had been in the New World for some time, and particularly in Minnesota with its great abundance of wheat, they soon learned to enjoy the flavor of all wheat bread. They learned through experimenting and through trial and error that leavening agents were floating all about their pioneer kitchens. They learned that by combining wheat flour, potatoe water and a sweetening agent that their bread became lighter and more palatable. Soon each kitchen had its "leavening pot" or its sour dough hidden within the flour barrel.

The following recipes have been taken from *The Delineator* 1896, Spring and Summer #4. Take note that none of these recipes call for salt, an important ingredient in today's recipes. Also, these cake recipes were used only after refined sugar was available and every well furnished kitchen had a stove-oven.

Raisin Cake-Two Large Loaves

1 large cupful of butter

2 cupfuls of sugar

1 cupful of milk

4 generous cupfuls flour

5 eggs

1 gill of brandy

2 nutmegs

1/2 teaspoon of salertus (soda)

1 quart of boiled raisins

Cook the raisins slowly for one-half hour, drain and cool. Beat the butter to a cream and beat the sugar into it. Add the brandy and grated nutmegs and beat again. Add the yolks of the eggs, well beaten. Dissolve the soda in the milk and add this to the beaten ingredients, add the flour. Stir in the well beaten egg whites. Spread the batter in thin layers in two large cake pans and sprinkle raisins over the batter. Continue to do this until all the materials are used up. Bake for two hours in a moderate stove-oven. This cake keeps well.

Angel Food Cake

To make an angel food cake take one cup flour, one and one-half cups refined sugar, eleven egg whites, one teaspoon extract, one teaspoon cream of tartar. Sift the flour four times, add cream of tartar and sift four more times. Sift the sugar through the flour sieve three times. Beat the egg whites to a stiff, dry froth. Add sugar a little at a time; add flour and extract. Do not butter the pan or oil the paper laid on the bottom. Bake slowly in a stove-oven about one hour. Place pan upside down until the cake falls out.

A Delicious Election Cake

1½ cupfuls of butter

1 cupful of currants

2 cupfuls of sugar

1/2 cupful of citron, chopped

1-1/2 pint flour

1/2 cupful of lemon peel ,chopped

1 teaspoon salertus (soda)

1/2 cupful of almond, shredded

1 teaspoon cream of tartar

20 drops of extract of bitter almonds

2 cupfuls raisins, stoned

20 drops of extract of vanilla

1 cupful of milk

Rub the butter and sugar to a thick cream add the eggs and beat a few minutes longer. Sift in the flour and cream of tartar, add the fruits, almond and extract and the milk in which the soda has been dissolved. Mix to a batter. Put paper into the bottom of a large pan and pour in the batter. Bake in a moderate stove-oven for one and one-half hours.

Pound Cake

For two large loaves, use two cupfuls of butter, two cupfuls of refined sugar, four cupfuls of flour, twelve large eggs, one-quarter teaspoonful of mace, one-half gill brandy. Butter the pans and line them. Measure the sugar, flour, mace and brandy. Separate the eggs putting the whites into a large bowl and the yokes into a small bowl. Beat the butter to a cream and gradually add the sugar to it. Add the brandy and mace. Beat the yolks until light and add to the mixture. Beat the whites to a froth and add them to the beaten mixture alternating with the flour. Pour into the pans and bake in a stove-oven about 50 minutes.

Yeast - How To Start as taken from Dr. Chases' Information For Everybody - Improved Edition - 1897.

Jug Yeast

Without yeast to start with, take hops (one-half pound), water (one gallon), fine malt flour (one-half pint), unrefined brown sugar (one-half pound). Boil the hops in the water until quite strong. Strain and stir in the malt flour and strain again through a coarse cloth. Boil again for ten minutes. When lukewarm stir in the sugar and pour into a jug, keeping it at the same warm temperature until it "works over." Then cork tight and keep in a cold place.

Yeast Cakes - How To Make

Good sized potatoes, one dozen; hops to one large handful; yeast, one-half pint (taken from the jug recipe). Peel and boil the potatoes and rub them through a colander. Boil the hops in two quarts of water, strain into the potatoes. Scald sufficient Indian cornmeal to make the consistency of "emptyings," stir in the yeast and let rise. Then with unscalded meal, thicken so as to roll out and cut into cakes. Dry quickly to prevent souring.

"Emptyings", as has been previously explained, were the settlings in a cider or beer keg. Malt flour was produced by drying and grinding or crushing the processed grain from breweries. It was also called malt dust.

CHAPTER XXII

Meat, Fowl and Fish On The Frontier

The early settlers were heavily dependant upon the Minnesota black bear for meat, lard, grease and hides. The black bear was no longer in plentiful supply, therefore, the pioneers did not wantonly slaughter the bear. The young males were used unless under dire necessity and want.

The Minnesota black hear was a source of meat and lard as a well fatted hog would have been. What pigs the settlers brought were saved as breeding stock. Not until their second year of grain production could they slaughter a hog for food. Besides oxen, only female beef animals were brought along, therefore, the black bear served them well.

The animal was skinned and the hides made into heavy coats, robes and rugs. All fat was carefully removed and rendered, and what was unpalatable for table use was used as grease. Combined with beeswax it made an excellent lubricant and water repellent for boots, moccasins and mittens, as well as for axle grease and wherever grease was needed on the frontier.

The organs and flesh were prepared and used much the same as pork is used. Of real value to the cook was the lard as it is difficult to prepare food without any shortening. Now the pioneer cook could prepare such delicacies as fried cakes, molasses ginger bread and other treats.

Wild fowl were plentiful and, therefore, was used during all seasons.

Early Settlers' Favorite Dinner

Any wild game was used, but the addition of chicken, pork or beef made the stew better. What meat was available was boiled until the meat was easily removed from the bones. This should amount to at least four pounds. Cut a dozen onions and several stalks of celery or cabbage in small pieces. Fry in a heavy skillet in one cup of lard until nicely browned, stirring so none will be scorched.

Into another skillet put another cup of lard, add the finely chopped meat and cook covered until tender on very low heat. Into a large deep kettle put several quarts of water, add salt and noodles to make a quart when done. Cook fifteen minutes. Add the cooked meat and vegetables, which should have been cooked only until they had a transparent look, add fat and all. Add dried or fresh mushrooms, or cooked lima beans and cooked tomatoes, of each about one pint. Add all the fat, drippings and fryings, and season to taste. Reheat but do not boil. Serve with hunks of French bread or hard rolls. Makes 10-12 servings.

Boiled Tongue With Vegetables

Scrub the tongue of the bear or beef well and parboil. Discard the water and add fresh water, boil until tender. Cool and remove the outer skin. Cut into thin slices, add a bay leaf, pepper and salt, and a bit of water; cover and stew gently until heated through. Add a pint of puree tomatoes, a pint of cooked diced carrots. Remove the bay leaf and add a large chopped onion, one-quarter cup butter and cook until the onions are done. Serve with boiled potatoes.

Ragout - The Frenchmen's Delicacy

Boil a mess of bear or pork hocks, add salt and a large chopped onion. When done cull and grind or chop the meat fine. Brown a cup of flour slowly in a heavy cast iron skillet; continuous stirring is necessary to prevent scorching. Form the meat into tiny balls, roll in the browned flour and fry until browned on all sides. Return the meat balls with the fryings to the liquid in the kettle and thicken it with the left-over browned flour dissolved in a bit of water. Season to taste and bring to a boil. Serve hot with boiled potatoes.

Head Cheese - Sylta

Clean and boil one hogs head or pigs hocks. Add salt, a bay leaf and an onion to the water and cook until the meat separates readily from the bones. Cool in the juice and remove the fat which has congealed on the top. Cut all the meat into bite sized pieces. Return the liquid to the kettle, add the meat and more seasoning, if necessary, and bring to a boil until all is well blended. Pour into convenient sized pans, cool thoroughly and chill. Cut into slices and serve cold.

Potatoes and Salt Pork

Slice and cut the pork into bite sized pieces. Soak in sour milk or plain warm water to remove some of the salt, wash and drain well. Fry it in a large heavy skillet along with three sliced onions, cooking gently until the onions are half cooked. Add raw thinly sliced potatoes sufficient for the meal. Season with pepper or other herbs, such as marjoram, cover and cook until the potatoes are half done. Turn the potatoes so the meat and onions are on top and finish cooking until done. Unless the potatoes are very mealy, there will be quite a bit of liquid in the skillet. Thicken this with two or three tablespoons flour blended with a bit of cold water. Stir this in gently and simmer until done. Serve hot.

Kropp Kakor

Boil four large potatoes, drain and mash. Peel and grate four raw potatoes and drain the surplus water through a cheese cloth bag (save this water for later). Add the grated potatoes to the boiled mashed potatoes. Add salt to taste and a bit of allspice, two eggs and mix well using just enough flour to form into balls.

Have enough cooked chopped meat to fill two cups. Brown this in a bit of butter and season with salt, pepper or marjoram.

If not enough liquid, add the potatoe water or plain hot water. Now, make a hole into each of the little dumplings and fill it with a spoonful of the meat mixture. Close the opening, adding flour if necessary, and drop one by one into the boiling broth. Use a large kettle and enough liquid so the dumplings can move freely as they cook. Cook rapidly for thirty minutes. Lift the cover and with a wooden spoon loosen any that may stick to the bottom. Cover and continue cooking for another hour or until done. Serve on a platter.

Before serving fry slender strips of bacon until golden and crispy. Pour bacon with the drippings over the dumplings, or melt butter and pour that over them.

This takes a lot of work, but it's as good today as it was when the early Scandinavians prepared it for their large families in the crowded log cabin homes.

Koldolmar - Another Scandinavian Dish

Boil a head of cabbage in water until the

leaves separate. Take a leaf at a time and fill with seasoned meat mixture. Roll carefully into a bundle and tie securely with string (string should have been boiled to shrink as well as to sterilize it). When the cabbage rolls are all filled and securely tied, brown them in melted butter or fat. Pour boiling water over them so the rolls are covered. Put a tight cover on the pan and cook for one and a half hours. Serve with buttered bread.

Meat mixture - Chop two cups cooked meat, mixtures of several meats are recommended, add one cup cooked rice, one-quarter cup sweet milk, one egg and a chopped onion. Season to taste, mix well, adding a bit of water if needed.

A Modern Version Of Pemmican

As good today as it was when the Klondike gold miners received it from the Indians in Alaska.

Use one part lean bear meat, one part

venison, one part poultry or lean beef, salt and seasonings to taste, pure lard or bear fat - two pounds to twenty pounds of meat used. Have ready muslin bags about six inches in diameter, boiled to shrink and sterilize, leaving them in the hot water until ready to use. Chop or grind the meat about medium fine. Season to taste and add water sparingly, only enough to start boiling. Cook over slow heat to prevent scorching. When tender, add berries. Finish cooking until done.

The Indians used pitted choke cherries, the cherries must have been larger than our Minnesota variety. Any berries or dried fruit may be used, but all seeds and stones must be removed.

Heat the lard or bear fat in a large deep kettle. It must be very hot, but do not let it come to a boil as it will foam, run over, and cause a messy situation as well as possible fire and burns. Ladle the meat carefully into the prepared bags. Pour the hot fat, ever so gently, into the bag so the fat will mingle with the meat as well as to seal the inside of the bag. Tie securely and cool at once. Kept in a cold place, it will keep for months. May be served as is or sliced and allowed to heat through which will remove some of the fat. A little goes a long way.

Booyah Fish Stew - By A French Canadian Trapper

Scale and clean a large fish. Strip the skin off so it remains in one piece without tears. Head should be left on - eyes and other foreign parts removed - washed and towel dried. Cook the fish in salted water until so tender that the meat can readily be removed from the bones, about twenty minutes. Mix the meat with hot mashed freshly boiled potatoes, season with salt and other condiments according to taste. Stuff the fish skin with the meat and potatoe mixture and tie securely with a string which has been boiled to prevent shrinkage as well as to sterilize it. Drop into the liquid in which the fish meat had been boiled. Cook only until thoroughly heated through. Serve as it comes from the kettle or brown it on all sides in a fry pan in a bit of butter or other fat. This gives it eye appeal. Served with a dish of coleslaw, it makes a meal.

Fish Soup - Polish Style

Clean the fish thoroughly, including the head. Remove the eyes and other foreign parts and all scales. Soak in cold water to which a little salt has been added for at least an hour. Then boil in water to which a bay leaf and one onion has been added.

The dear friend who gave us this recipe said, "One large fish is better than several small ones." She added, "Fish soup without the fish's head has no flavor."

When the meat can be easily picked off the bones, remove it and strain the liquid through a fine sieve or cloth so any bones will be removed. Pour the strained liquid back into the pot. Add the meat with an equal amount of raw sliced potatoes, a minced onion and salt and pepper. Bring to a boil.

Dice bacon strips, one to each person, and fry -- do not fry over low heat. When browned, stir a spoonful of flour into the fat and bacon, cook until well blended. Add cold water or milk slowly to make a smooth sauce. Add this to the soup pot, reheat and remove from the fire. Add a cup of thin cream or two cups of milk.

Bakt Loks - Baked Trout

Clean one large fish. Sprinkle inside and out with salt and stuff with a filling made of four cups dry bread crumbs, one-half cup melted fat drippings or sausage fryings, pinch salt and one of sage. Bake about one hour.

Bakt Rokt Fisk - Baked Smoked Fish

Use five fat smoked fish. Skin, clean and remove all bones. Cut in small pieces, place into deep pan and cover with cream, sweet or sour. Bake till done, about twenty minutes. Good with boiled potatoes.

Stewed Terrapin Or Water Turtle

Plunge the terrapins into boiling water, let them remain until the sides and the bottom shell begin to crack. This will take an hour or more depending upon size. Remove and allow to cool. Carefully remove the shell and save any oozing blood. If the terrapin has eggs, remove them so as not to puncture the skins. Remove all the entrails being careful not to break the gallbladder -- discard this. Save the liver and cut it up with the rest of the meat adding the blood and any other juices which have been saved. Place it all into a deep pan, sprinkle a bit of flour over all, add about a cup of water, salt, pepper, a dash of cayenne pepper and mace. Allow to simmer over a slow fire, covered. Shortly before serving add a cup of cream, a fourth pound of butter and the skinned turtle eggs. Simmer until the eggs are cooked. This recipe is for four turtles.

The eggs of the terrapin were highly sought by our pioneer women. They went out on egg hunts in late summer or early fall when hen eggs and those of wild fowl were scarce. The eggs were used in cooking and baking the same as hen eggs.

Pickled Fish - Carp Or Other Rough Fish

The fish are stripped of their skin and the large backbone removed. The remainder is cut into suitable pieces and soaked in cold water to which a handful of pure salt has been added to remove all traces of blood and impurities. An hour is sufficient, then drain and wash in clear water.

The pieces are then placed into a stoneware baking crock having a tight fitting cover. Over each layer of fish slices of onions, a bay leaf, and fresh or dried peppers are scattered. When the crock is nearly filled, pure hot vinegar is poured. A teaspoon of salt and one of sugar is added. Place the cover on the crock and set into a medium oven to bake five hours or until the bones are soft so they may be eaten along.

Our cooks on the frontier had no oven so they placed the crock into the cast iron kettle, filled it with water and hung it upon the heavy hook within the fireplace where she cooked all her meals. If she had no cover for her stone crock, she made a dough of flour and water and rolled it to the desired size. She spread it over the top so it extended an inch or so down the sides, pressing it down firmly. The heat of the crock soon cooked it into an airtight cover.

Boiled Calf's Head -

As Taken From An Old Cookbook

Put the head into boiling water and let it remain about five minutes. Take it out, hold it by the ear, and with the back of a knife scrape off all the hair. When perfectly clean, take out the eyes, cut off the ears and remove the brain, which is soaked for an hour in hot water. Put the head to soak in hot water a few minutes to make it look white. Have ready a deep pan in which to lay the head, cover with cold water and put it gradually to boil. Add a little salt which makes the scum rise to the top so it can be skimmed off. When the head is cooked so tender that the meat separates from the bone, take it out of the pan and drain it.

Score the top and spread melted butter over it, dredge it with flour, sprinkle with salt and pepper, and set into a hot oven to brown. Serve it with a bowl of melted butter and minced parsley.

Boil the brains, which have been soaking in cold water, for fifteen minutes. Skin and chop them, add a tablespoon of minced parsley, which has been previously scalded, stir in four table-spoons of melted butter and serve along with the calf's head as a side dish.

The brains of the animal are properly called the sweet breads and are considered a delicacy when properly prepared.

Stewed Rabbit, Squirrel And Chipmunk

Wash the skinned game in warm water, soak in cold water to which a tablespoon of pure salt has been added. Cut the game into suitable sized pieces. Place into a stew pot and add two cups cold water, a bunch of sweet herbs, an onion minced, a pinch of mace, half a nutmeg, a pinch of pepper and half a pound of salt pork cut into thin slices. Cover and stew until tender. When done, take out the meat and keep it warm. Add to the gravy in the pot a cup of cream or milk, two well beaten eggs stirred in slowly, a tablespoon of butter and thickening made of a tablespoon flour with a little milk. Boil up once. Pour this over the meat and serve with onion sauce.

Stewed Frogs

Wash and skin the quarters and parboil for three minutes. Drain and place them into a stew pan with four tablespoons butter, fry gently so both sides are browned. Sift a little flour over the meat and a sprig of parsley, a pinch of powdered savory, a bay leaf, three slices of onion, salt and pepper, a cup of hot water and one of cream, cover and stew until done. Remove the meat and strain the juices. Return to the pot and thicken with the yolks of two well beaten eggs, stirred slowly into the gravy. Pour this over the meat and serve.

CHAPTER XXIII

Beverages - Substitutes For

Coffee and tea as we know them today were unknown to the settlers on the frontier. A good hot brew was a must and, again, it was up to the pioneer woman to come up with the wherewithal to brew a stout pot of refreshments. Herbs grew plentifully and were gathered and dried in season. The blossoms of the basswood tree were used and roots were washed, dried and roasted. Vegetable and fruit parings were dried and roasted. The kernel of acorns were dried and

218

roasted. Chicory was planted for the purpose but did not do well in our climate. Even bread crusts were browned over coals and crushed and boiled in water to produce a pot of hot coffee.

As soon as grain was produced barley was found to be superior to all else for a delicious, healthful beverage. The following recipe has been used in the family of this writer until the good, reliable wood burning oven was replaced with an electric stove.

The barley was carefully hand cleaned so there was not the least chance that a weed seed could be missed, which would produce an off flavor for the entire batch. It was then washed through many water changes and left to soak in warm water until tiny sprouts appeared. The sprouted barley was carefully washed again and spread out to dry on clean cloths. When the grain felt just right to the cook she gathered it into shallow pans about an inch deep. It was then placed in the sun, usually on a low roof top. By night, or when the sun was overcast, it was brought indoors. Frequent stirring was necessary.

After the kitchens had cookstoves with ovens the roasting was done in the oven. This required up to three days of diligent care and watchfulness. Prior to that the roasting was done in long handled covered pans over the coals in the fireplace. Museums and antique shows refer to these pans as popcorn poppers, but their original use was as roasters.

To roast and not to scorch took an experienced hand and was often done by the husband during the long winter evenings while the wife was knitting, or spinning, or perhaps even weaving the flax to make a new garment. The freshly roasted coffee was then allowed to cool thoroughly and then stored in tin cans. If none were available, the settlers soon learned through their Indian neighbors the art of how to make beautiful, serviceable containers from the bark of the birch tree or from reeds.

To brew a cup of coffee the kernels were ground in a hand mill or mashed with a wooden stomper. Long boiling was required to bring out the truly rich flavor of the roasted barley kernels. Tea drinkers found ample supplies of nature's herbs and roots to quench their thirst. In every locality some herbs of the wild variety are still to be found in abundance. What must it have been like when the early settlers found the land in its wild primitive beauty and splendor.

The wild strawberry was a favorite, camille came next in flavor, but the strong growthy plant of the comfry was the working man's standby. Even three thousand years ago the comfry was highly regarded by the Greeks as a beverage and still is used for its medicinal propertics.

The Indians generously shared their knowledge of the common herbs and roots with the settlers. They taught them how to select the plants at the proper time and how to handle them after harvesting. They taught them that the common dandelion produced a strong bitter tea while the roots, after drying and roasting, produced a likeable coffee substitute.

Wild rose hips and the wild mulberry when dried made a tasty tea. Although they knew nothing of vitamins, the tea of the rose and mulberry hips very likely saved them from outbreaks of developing scurvy during the long, lean winter months.

The long, dark Minnesota winters with the cabins lighted only by tallow candles were certainly cheered by steaming mugs of herb tea, perhaps sweetened by wild honey or maple sugar, all of which had been garnered during the summer months by the family.

CHAPTER XXIV

Our Nations Calamities
From 1770 Through The 1870's

Historical records indicate that ever since the white man established residence in America, this nation suffered through a decade of calamities once each century.

The calamities which befell our nation at the end of the civil war brought far reaching after effects to our young state of Minnesota. By then the southern part of our state and all the land east of the Mississippi River were fast progressing in an orderly fashion of that period. The rich virgin land was producing well and settlers were replacing their original sod or log cabins with frame buildings. Cities and industries had become a fast growing fact. As debts were paid with cheap money, adventurers gambled on borrowed money.

At the end of 1872 the state had approximately 2,000 miles of railroad in operation. Much of this money came from the largest bank in the nation, the Jay Cooke Bank of New York. It was beyond comprehension that a man of Jay Cooke's great wealth and managerial ability could "go broke". Like Humpty Dumpty he fell and the crash was heard around the world, although it took a while for the news to make the rounds. It triggered the panic of 1873. This vast expanse of railroad was built to serve as links in a transcontinental system of transportation.

Our sparsely populated central and northwest regions could not support its share in revenue producing tonnage in view of the harsh fact, which was not taken into consideration by the planners. A greater time was required to clear this rough land to produce grains and livestock beyond the needs of local consumption.

When the news broke about the Jay Cooke Bank of New York, it brought immediate concern and even despair to every town along the Northern Pacific. Duluth, which had a population of 5,000 collapsed practically overnight. These people had invested in good faith that the railroad would bring untold income from trade from the west coast and even overseas. Within a few weeks the population had dwindled down to 1,300. It was a long and very difficult struggle until they could begin to pay their indebtedness. Duluth took the full force of the panic of 1873.

After the Civil War, bank failures were the rule among the banks in the Union. However, Minnesota was in better financial condition to withstand the crash. By the end of the war Minnesota had thirteen incorporated banks. By July 1864 all banks had agreed to accept only "lawful money of the United States", no out of state currency was accepted. By 1866 Minnesota had sixteen national banks in operation. After the war Congress had imposed a 10%. tax on all state banks, therefore, all state banks had surrendered their privileges. Consequently, most of the money had the backing of the United States Government. Greenbacks had become depreciated and were accepted only at a discount.

The Seegar Impeachment

Prompted by the extravagance and corruption which brought about the failures of the railroads and the banking businesses all over the nation, citizens everywhere urged investigations into their own state affairs. Soon disclosures were made that the State Treasurer's Office in St. Paul was not in proper order. A St. Paul newspaper challenged this statement and rumors spread like wild fire.

Consequently, a committee was appointed to investigate the Treasurer's Office. Evidence was presented that when William Seegar took office in January 1872 there was an actual deficit of $120,000. Mr. Seegar had not only concealed this fact but made loans of nearly $750,000, keeping the interest for his own use. He had also induced various County Treasurers to advance large sums to deceive investigators.

The Governor was asked to resign, but refused; therefore, the House brought charges of impeachment accusing him with high crimes and misdemeanors while in office. This brought Seegar to file his resignation, but the impeachment proceedings went on nevertheless. Seegar was found guilty on all counts, removed from office, and disqualified from ever again holding any public office.

Because the state did not suffer any financial losses, it was decided that if the Treasurer had been paid an adequate salary he might not have been tempted to embezzle public funds. The Treasurer's salary was $1,000 per year. To prevent any future misuse the legislature raised the salary to $3,500 per year.

Emil Munch, Seegar's son-in-law, was connected with this scandal; therefore, he too was charged with the same offence along with Seegar.

Minnesotans, wherever they may have lived, remembered the year of 1873 for a long, long time; not only for the great panic that hit mostly the moneyed people, but for the "great snow" that practically buried them along with their livestock when the heavy January snows began to fall. Hundreds lost their lives and many more suffered permanent injuries, not only because of the frost and cold, but due to malnutrition.

The spring was late in coming as the great depth of snow and ice melted so slowly that many fields could not be planted that season. In early October another blizzard came with ice and snow drifts which covered all fall crops, their wood for fuel, as well as their meager supplies of hay and fodder for their livestock. Suffering and desolation prevailed over much of the central and northwest counties. Spring brought outbreaks of contagious diseases taking many more lives.

Due to the heavy accumulations of compacted snow and ice, the spring was late again. Crops, however, were planted in dry spots giving new hope to the settlers. The many soft spots and pot holes filled with stagnant water became ideal breeding grounds for mosquitoes and insects which had never been seen before in this new land.

Suddenly, in the heat and humidity of July, great black hordes of the Montana locusts came sweeping into the state devouring everything that was planted by man. The native grasses remained untouched, but their eggs were laid in these sheltered spots. Some areas were a total loss while others reaped at least seeds for the following year.

The year of 1874 was, by far, the worst for the pioneers as the locusts had taken everything from as far north as Canada and far into the state of Texas. The locusts had crossed the Mississippi and the entire state was now affected. Fortunately, the state had a surplus from the previous good years so all were given who needed it.

This brought renewed courage to the farmers. However, as the seeds sprouted and set up their fragile green stems so, also, had the locust eggs hatched bringing hordes of a new and hardier breed of hungry locusts. The insects provided rich protein feed for wildlife, fowls and pigs, but no grain was saved that year.

The farmers frantically made attempts to destroy them by burning their stubble fields before plowing and tried various other methods available to them. That year, however, twenty-eight counties were ravaged. Settlers were abandoning their farms and homes to move to areas where the locusts were still unknown.

Want and poverty stalked our young state of Minnesota. In 1874 General Sibley took charge of relief work. He appointed a committee to study the habits of the locusts and to travel to remote counties to learn conditions and needs.

In spite of all this, the year of 1875 was the severest of the decade. Even where the locusts had not been, the wheat crop was a miserable failure due to weather conditions bringing new plant diseases. What was harvested was of inferior quality.

In the year of 1876-7 the locusts had invaded areas where they had not been before. This brought statewide scarcities in food. As the wheat was ripe for the reaper, the locusts arrived in black hordes so thick that they darkened the skies as would a thunder cloud devouring in minutes what it had taken a year to produce.

In 1878 a program for exterminating this plague was established by the legislature. $100,000 was allocated for bounty on the locusts. Hot tar was poured into breeding places and scrapers were invented with attachments for oil to be spread upon the hatching areas. Some were crushed and millions killed in various ways until the funds ran out, but the locust eggs continued to hatch new and hardier hordes of locusts. Governor Pillsbury used his own money and begged from his friends for help, but year after year the plague spread further along.

The spring of 1879 was not one of hope and optimism, but one of want, hunger and devastation all over the state. After the Governor had personally visited as many areas as he could, he did a somewhat unusual thing... or was it the most natural? This religiously inspired man proclaimed April 26th as a day of prayer. He called upon the people to lay aside their burdens and labors, repair their houses of worship and ask God for deliverance from this evil.

During the following night the weather turned so cold that it brought the hardest frost ever recorded for that date. Dead locusts were found in heaps all over the land. The plague was over and has not returned to this day.

How would we, in this day of 1977, deal with such hardships and privations? (The state would be declared a disaster area and aid would come...or so we are believing!)

The foregoing article has been gleaned from the *History Of Minnesota* by Theodore Christianson, L.L.D.

"A pioneer Minnesota farm wife had invented an implement drawn by hand or horse power which greatly reduced the locust infestation in the 1870's. The invention simply called for a strip of sheet iron turned up at each side and at the front. A light weight chain was attached to each side on the front end and as the skid was dragged along the field, the chain hustled the locusts from the stubble into the sheet iron skid which was painted over with heavy tar. This served as a trap which was pulled across the fields. When filled, the mass of locusts were scraped off and burned." (Inventor's name unknown.)

CHAPER XXV

Log House Construction

The rules given here apply to all Scandinavian built log cabins of that early period as taken from the book by Mr. Arnold Greften of Wanaaska, Minnesota entitled *The Land Of Howling Wolves* (with his permission).

Mr. Arnold Greften explains that it took one team of horses to skid a trimmed tamarack log out of the forest. A team of two horses was hitched to a singletree about three feet long. Each singletree was fastened to each end of the doubletree, which was shaped out of a sound oak tree into a piece of board four and one-half feet long, five inches wide, by two and one-half inches. Into the exact center of this doubletree the clevis was fastened to which two log chains were attached. Each of the chains was hooked to either end of the tree. The teamster was now able to skid the log to the site of the new home. He continued to skid the logs in as fast as two men in the forest could fell and trim them

Other neighbors were busy at the building site shaping the logs with their broad axes into perfect squares of twelve inch in diameter building logs. This process also removed all the bark. Some builders left the outer side of the log in its naturally rounded shape. The logs were notched at each end and fitted so perfectly that the finished building was airtight. As the building progressed, one man worked inside to hew and even the logs so the resulting wall would be smooth and clean. To secure the logs, two inch holes were drilled into the log above and partway into the log below. Then a hand carved wooden plug was driven firmly into the opening. This was done particularly around the window and door openings.

When the building had progressed to the height above the windows, eight inch diameter logs were used until the cabin was of the desired height. This was usually twelve feet, which allowed for a loft. In case of a single room cabin, six to seven feet was sufficient. Three windows and one door opening was considered proper, a window on each side and one on the wall near the door. This was considered a day's work for the crew. The following day was given for the construction of the roof.

To do this, twenty-six by fourteen inch tamarack timber was selected, trimmed, scaled of its bark, then skidded to the building site. This was for the ridge pole and was skidded in to lie sixteen feet away from the wall. Four more six inch poles, twenty feet in length, were placed into a slanting position with one end resting on top of the uppermost log and the other end firmly into the ground. One was placed at each end of the cabin and the other two evenly spaced between these two. A log chain was attached to each end of the log and one team was hitched to each chain. The trick was now for the teamsters to pull evenly and very slowly, while watching each other's team as well as their own, to slide the ridge pole to the top of the building. This task done, they measured out the exact spot where the ridge pole was to be.

Poles five inches by ten feet in length were used for the roof. These were laid from the center of the ridge pole and extended about a foot over the wall. The ends resting against the ridge pole were drilled through and into the ridge pole and secured with a wooden plug. This held them solidly in place. The roof was hewed and smoothed to make it as airtight as possible.

But it still must be covered with shingles. This item was usually not to be had on the frontier. The builders returned to the forest to strip bark from the giant birches which were found in every forest and around every pot hole. The strips were cut into even length; but of varying widths, so placed that they always overlapped one another. Strips of sod were placed over the birch strips to keep them in position and from being blown off by the wind.

The cabin was now finished except for the windows, a door and a floor, but these three items were considered needless luxuries. As it was usually a weeks' trip to the nearest town the pioneers made it no oftener than was necessary, which was in spring and fall. Then a caravan was formed of no less than three wagons loaded with whatever they had to barter in exchange for what they needed in the way of staples, seed, medication or, in this case, a door and three windows.

Meanwhile, the pioneers used a huge bear hide for a door and scraps of cloth dipped into a hot mixture of fat with a bit of beeswax added for their windows. When dry it kept out most of the rain and wind as well as the precious sunlight.

Dirt floors were the rule in the pioneer's home. By the constant patter of bare feet and daily sweeping they soon became as hard as concrete. Tanned bear hides were spread over them in the winter. The brooms also came from the forest. Slender willows were cut into two foot lengths fastened to one end of a pole with wire, if it was available, otherwise with cord cut from a pelt. About halfway down, the willow switches were again firmly tied. This made a very sturdy broom for the dirt floors or, when coarse wide planks were used, for flooring.

As the fresh cut logs dried they also shrank somewhat. To remedy any leaks in the walls, they were plastered before freeze-up with a mixture made out of a sticky clay gumbo. When dry it could be whitewashed.

This rounds out that period of our state in which the log cabins and sod shanties constituted the main source for shelter for man, his family, as well as for his animals. It is unfortunate that so few have been preserved for posterity. The reason may be that all were constructed with minimum labor, at no cost and without solid foundations, merely set upon the ground itself where rot and decay soon set in to do their job to destroy. Preservatives were unknown. Had they been available, the cost would have played a factor against their use. Nevertheless, as the cabins were constructed of newly hewn logs fresh from the forests, the homeowners displayed great pride in them. The cabins and soddies afforded comfort, warmth and neighborliness. Large families were born, nurtured and grew into adulthood. Marriages were performed and weddings were held in cabins far less pretentious than the one described here. Wakes were also held, far too many in the early days.

But, for any reason, or no reason whatsoever, an impromptu jamboree was arranged where the furniture was hoisted to the rafters or put on pegs on the walls. Anyone who had a fiddle, accordion or mouth organ would strike up a lively tune, which would set all to dancing throughout the night.

Mary Joos

by Helen Joos Cichy

BIOGRAPHY

Give a little girl a needle, a length of colored thread and a scrap of cloth and you have given her a way of life.

Such was the case when early Minnesotans struggled to bring civilization to the west central counties of our state.

Mary Klein Joos was born in 1873 to Antoine Klein and Helena Voelker Klein in Carlos township. Along with an older and a younger brother the small family moved to Millerville, Douglas County, in I 879, having purchased the Frank Weber homestead which is now in the ownership of Herbert Haiden, a great-grandson of Helena.

The family made this move so the children who would soon be of school age could attend a school within walking distance. Proper starting age was considered to be eight or nine years of age, terms ran from six to seven months.

The first school in Millerville was a small frame building located on church grounds. Qualified parents were the first teachers in this school, which was the first school for the Klein children, their neighbors, as well as for the entire community.

In 1882, a new frame church was constructed in Our Lady of Seven Dolors Parish, then considered the most beautiful spacious church edifice in Douglas County.

That fall three Benedictine nuns came from St. Joseph to establish a new school in the old log church. The loft of this building was used as their dwelling place.

Nine-year old Mary and her older brother were delighted with this fine new school and their teacher. Besides regular classes, they taught needlecraft to the girls and woodcraft to the boys.

Mary soon outdid all her classmates in sewing and crocheting. Her teacher was so pleased with her that she invited Mary to come for further training on weekends and holidays.

By the time Mary reached her thirteenth birthday her school days were over and she did most of the family's sewing by hand.

She was hired out then as a housemaid to a family who owned and operated a general merchandise store in Parkers Prairie, Minnesota.

After her sewing talents became known she spent most of her time recycling the garments the older members had outgrown or discarded into new garments for their siblings. Part of Mary's wages was cast off garments which the oldest daughter, a schoolteacher, no longer wanted. Also, by accepting castoffs, she had more and better quality garments than she could have had otherwise. Besides, she had the opportunity to examine the sewing of an experienced seamstress and thereby correct her own way. In no way did Mary feel humiliated or resentful of this as it was considered right and proper for parents to collect the earnings of their children below legal age.

By eighteen and of legal age, Mary was in the employ of a professional seamstress, Mrs. Sontag of Alexandria, Minnesota, who owned a fine sewing machine. This was the first sewing machine Mary had ever seen. The fascination, which developed between Mrs. Sontag and her magnificent machine and Mary somehow became lost in the events, which soon followed.

A dormant dream in Mary's maturing mind was taking shape. The longing to be an accomplished dressmaker owning her very own sewing machine became overwhelming. Her prudent upbringing told her to forget this and keep her mind on the work she was paid to do. Now, at last, she was earning money for her work, which was doing the housework so Mrs. Sontag could spend full time at her sewing machine.

There comes a time in the lives of most young people when they fantasize about a home of their own with a mate and where all things become possible. For some time the young man in Mary's life had been waiting for her to become serious concerning his proposal of marriage. Up to this point she had only known him as an escort to the church dinner in Alexandria, and he wasn't bad on the dance floor, either. He could even take the place of one of the musicians who furnished the music.

Fredrick Joos could not imagine his young bride as a dressmaker, much as he admired Mrs. Sontag who had been as a second mother to him since he arrived in Douglas County He had found work with Mr. Sontag who was a dealer in real estate and horses.

Mary couldn't see her husband as a professional dealer in horses either, but they compromised by marrying. Later on, as they became more as one, they would be in a better position to work out their future together.

Mrs. Sontag sewed Mary's wedding dress

along with all the accessories, even her matching fingerless gloves. The fabric for this once in a lifetime ensemble was soft, all wool cashmere in deep beige, referred to as "buckskin" in 1892.

Immediately after the wedding the young couple took the train to St Paul where Fredrick's family was located throughout the suburban area. The train ride was a first for Mary as was meeting his family. All were established families with his widowed mother living with a daughter and family.

Mary felt immature, inexperienced, and even a bit uncouth in manner and speech, which made her fresh innocence even more pronounced. Fredrick, being very proud of his little bride, decided to take her to Arlington where his widowed sister owned and operated her own millinery and dressmaking shop. This was a fortunate decision. Here, Mary felt comfortable with her sister-in-law, Bertha Roth, and Bertha's two young sons who lost no time in making Mary feel accepted. They reminded Mary of her two young brothers on their farm in far away Millerville.

Bertha, a talented seamstress, could not fail to see the latent creativity Mary had in all branches of needlecraft. Therefore, she suggested that Fredrick might take his little bride to visit Mrs. Mary Malloy She operated a sewing school in St. Paul at Forepaugh and West Seventh Street

Mary found Mrs. Malloy to be a kind, generous person of Irish descent with whom she soon felt able to talk about her secret dream with the sewing machine. The visit ended with Mary's enrollment in the sewing school. Fredrick promised to change residency to St. Paul as soon as he could find a suitable apartment. Living quarters for the couple would have to be within walking distance of the school. He paid her tuition that day.

After Mary had completed her course she and her husband returned to Arlington. This is where their first child, a son, was born. Even with a new baby to love and care for, Mary was restless to start. her dressmaking shop. it con-tinued to be an important factor in the lives of this couple.

Mary wanted to be with her family and friends. She felt that they needed her services much more than anyone in Arlington where there were several established shops already

In the spring of 1898 the little family moved to Millerville. There they purchased a lot with a small house and other buildings as was required in that day to provide for a family life style.

A fine modern sewing machine was among the modest furnishings they brought along. No sooner were they settled in their new home, which proved to be their only home for the rest of their lives, than Mary was receiving more clients than she could care for.

In November, their second child, another son, was born. He died at five months of age. The sudden death of this seemingly healthy child destroyed the joy and hopes in their new home.

Mary became inconsolable, blaming herself for not having given the infant sufficient care. Her sewing machine remained closed and her work piled up. Fredrick, feeling trapped and helpless in the new community, began to spend his time in the local tavern, instead of caring for the carpentry trade he had already developed. He felt the baby's death by croup and pneumonia could have been prevented if he had provided a better home for his family.

The black clouds of grief and sorrow passed on. On another early spring morning their first infant daughter was born. Fredrick was overjoyed. Now he knew that the good Lord no longer blamed him for carelessness toward his child. Right then he decided that the small home must be enlarged, modernized and made comfortable.

By the time the old century had given way to the twentieth, the family was comfortable in their spacious home, which included one large room on the first floor for Mary's sewing room and dressmaking shop.

No longer was she a timid, unsure country girl, but a matron who knew how to proceed toward the safe fulfillment of her destiny.

Soft spoken and resourceful, Mary worked hard, managing their new home and caring for their two young children. Like everyone else they raised a garden, fed chickens, had a pig or two as well as a cow to supply themselves with food that was otherwise not available.

By late summer she had opened her dress-making shop. She made it known that she accepted students as well. Her spacious, well-lighted room was centered with a long oaken table, handcrafted by her older brother as a gift. Mary's precious sewing machine was stationed nearby in front of a large window. This is where it, or a new replacement, remained for the 35 years her shop was in operation.

Mirrors of various sizes and shapes were on all walls. Beside each minor was a bracket lamp, and, being they were kerosene burning, required daily care. A beautiful chandelier fastened to the ceiling operated with brass pulleys, chains and other accessories. The lamp required frequent polishing but little care otherwise as all it ever gave off was black sooty smoke instead of light. Hand lamps were on every table, night stand or dresser, with the finest one in back of the sewing machine on the window sill. This is where Mrs. Joos could be found every night until midnight, except Sundays and holidays.

Small tables were piled high with quarterly fashion plates in black and white (color plates were still a ways off). Many of the magazines were discards from Mrs. Malloy's St. Paul shop.

THE DRESSMAKER'S CHART

The First requisite for the dressmaker was the ability to design her own patterns. Ready-made tissue paper patterns, as we know them now, were not available in the early 1900's. Neither were ready-made ladies' and children's garments.

To design and fit her patterns, the trained, experienced seamstress used a set of charts, crafted out of lightweight wood board which had to be blemish free. The wood board was then sanded and polished. A set of charts consisted of three parts. Part one was shaped to form the front of a garment, part two as die back and part three for a sleeve similar to patterns used today. All edges were gauged and numbered similar to a cabinet maker's precision tools.

How-to instructions were applied with black paint in English and foreign languages as well. A small booklet came with each chart giving detailed instructions on how to design current fashions.

It was a simple matter for Mrs. Joos to design any pattern style her clients requested. Her quarterly fashion plate supplied instructions for current styles.

By working right along with the students, Mrs. Joos taught them the vital importance of always using a tape measure with the chart to give each garment correct fit without waste of materials and time.

Some students came so poorly educated in reading and arithmetic that they could only be taught though memorizing. These girls seldom learned the art of designing a pattern. Still they learned how to assemble the different parts and

sew them into serviceable garments for themselves and their families.

STYLE AND DESIGN

A woman did not have closets full of
dresses that were almost new. She felt fortunate if
she had one good dress for special occasions. To
design, cut, assemble and sew a dress required
many hours of skillful hand labor as well as machine labor.

Practically every garment was lined, and
inner linings were even added in some finely
woven fabrics. Stays of whalebone or buckram
were tacked between linings in collars, cuffs, and
belts. Basques, which were high fashion for many
years, had whalebone supports the length of every
seam while bustles were supported with buckram.
Sleeves were pulled, shined or tucked as fashion
demanded, while those floor sweeping skirts had
up to fourteen gores, each fully lined. The wide
flaring bottom was reinforced with 12 inch bands
of buckram to which brush-like braid was sewn.
This served as protection against wear and tear of
walking on dirt, gravel and other hazards to long

wearing garments.

Hooks and eyes were sewn in long even rows to front or back garment closings, while more rows of ornamental buttons were attached as decor. Tiny colorful glass beads were attached to the fronts of ladies' dresses in attractive decorative designs. Glittering jet spangles were used in the same manner, all attached by hand using the smallest size needles available. The completed garment was a work of art.

Mrs. Joos, with the assistance of her students, created many such garments for all sizes and ages. Her clients came from long distances. As they brought only a yardage of dress material, it was always up to her to supply all the extras to produce the finished garment. In the beginning this was all ordered from St. Paul. Small quantities arrived by mail, while larger orders were delivered by costly express or slow-moving freight. Fortunately, it was at this time that Anthony J. Lorsung and a brother purchased the Kotchevar store in Millerville. The brothers soon dissolved the partnership, with Anthony and his wife retaining full control.

After some remodeling, the store became a fully stocked general mercantile business. Not only were the shelves stocked with a good variety of fabrics but they contained sewing necessities as well. Shoppers could now select what they wanted with the efficient help of Mrs. Lorsung, but many continued to rely on Mrs. Joos to "buy what was right." From then on Mrs. Joos placed her seasonal orders with the Lorsungs. For the first time she could fill customer needs as they arose, without waiting for orders to arrive.

A visiting client was taken by Mr. Joos into her parlor. This was a small nicely furnished room where the latest fashion plates were invitingly open on the center table. Here the client would open her parcel and tell Mrs. Joos what to make out of the material she had brought. The client usually had a vague plan in her mind, which she could not explain until she had seen a similar item in one of the fashion plates.

Mrs. Joos was well versed in German and English but some of her clients spoke neither of these languages. They were immigrants who spoke only their languages which may have been

Polish, Swedish, Norwegian and other dialects. But Mrs. Joos was a gifted person in understanding. She had no difficulty in communicating with anyone who came to her. There were times when she would take them into her kitchen. There was almost nothing that could not be settled over a cup of coffee and a sandwich.

After all the decisions were completed, Mrs. Joos took careful measurements which she kept in her small note book. She would then ask her client for her signature. This was necessary because she could seldom pronounce their foreign names and much less, spell them. All of the transactions remained between her and her client. Students or family members were never permitted to these sessions. It is assured that Mrs. Joos never made an enemy. All continued to give her their patronage or visit as dear friends. They brought their daughters not only to have dresses made in the latest fashion for growing girls, but also for advice on how to treat acne, and care of their hair, which their mothers taught them to keep under control with liberal applications of goose grease, and other such up-to-date advice.

Through her sewing shop and school, Mrs. Joos formed a connecting link in which immigrant women could raise their children in American life styles. It was difficult for an adult to learn a second language and some found it impossible. Mrs. Joos never learned to speak in any foreign language except German, which she learned as a child. Her deep will to learn to communicate instinctively led her into an unusual affinity of making language unnecessary, and certainly no barrier.

The chart Mrs. Joos was so dependant on helped her not only in sewing but with the how-to instructions being printed in several foreign languages in addition to English and German. The chart became a handy interpreter.

In later years, when tissue paper became readily available, she was often called upon to design costumes for talent plays or other entertainment. Live entertainment was all that was known in those days, and this was when her chart came into use again and again.

The students always enjoyed cutting the

fabric for these costumes. Errors could easily be corrected or overlooked since these garments were frequently for one time wear only, after which they were made into other wearable garments. Though these experiences the students learned about art and craft work and how to furnish and beautify their future homes.

Wedding gowns and complete ensembles for the bride and her maids were made. First communion, confirmation outfits as well as complete layettes for the newly born, and, yes, even shrouds for the deceased were sewn in Mrs. Joos' school and shop. Undoubtedly, their busiest season was from Lent through Easter extending through the Fourth of July.

For this national holiday a new, brightly colored, frilly dress was a must for every lady, little girl, teenager or any girl of dancing age. Each student was encouraged to sew her own dress. With the supervision of Mrs. Joos, it was always a perfect creation. How proud they were! By the end of this busy season the six month course had also ended. While some returned for an occasional course later on, it marked the end of any further training, for the majority of students. They invariably married but returned for further help as they needed it and it was always given freely.

In Mrs. Joos' sewing school first lessons began by threading a needle and tying a neat secure knot at the longer end. Keeping a thimble on the student's second finger of her right hand, if they were right handed, was a must. This last was a difficult lesson for some to learn but breaking this rule was not condoned. There was no punishment given but students were reminded several times until they followed this rule.

Early sewing machines were so simply and sturdily constructed that the only thing that could break was the needle. Beginners broke so many that Mrs. Joos ordered them by multi-gross. To replace the needle was a painstaking task for the beginner. After having been shown how, she was expected to follow printed instructions. Nevertheless, it usually took several broken needles and more tear-mingled sessions before this lesson was learned.

The shop had an extra sewing machine or

two for beginners' training sessions. Rarely, if ever, was anyone privileged to use Mrs. Joos' machine. This precious item was replaced every fifth year with a new one while her old machine was moved over to the beginners' side of the shop.

Any of these machines could be purchased by the students at low cost, and usually were. Lessons learned by doing were seldom forgotten while proverbs were used wherever applicable. Instructors in schools had generous supplies stored in the files of their minds' reaches.

The capacity of Mrs. Joos' sewing class was four students although she had as many as six at one time. Four were boarders who assisted with housework after or before class in payment for room and board. Others would be day-students who were required to pay a small tuition, which was usually an exchange for farm produce.

Students were treated as members of the family. In the kitchen they were taught meal preparation off the farm, canning, baking and correct table setting. Along with table manners, these things received even more appreciation from the students than the good food that was served in Mrs. Joos' dining room.

Many of these bright young ladies were so shy and sensitive of their foreign background that they found it difficult to answer simple questions. Away from home and family for the first time, they were lonely, homesick and needed encouragement to learn and finish their courses.

Mrs. Joos saw herself in these girls not so many years ago when she was taken to Parkers Prairie to work for strangers. Still later she recalled how awkward she felt in the presence of Mrs. Malloy in her sewing school in St. Paul until this kind Irish instructor took her into her confidence.

By applying much the same technique with her students, Mrs. Joos helped them overcome their problems simply by bringing them out. Some of the girls were sensitive regarding their hair, old-fashioned homemade clothes, or worst of all, their acne.

Most of life's problems were caused by language barriers. Unless one understood the true intended meaning of the person speaking, his or her words could be totally ineffective or meaningless. What was needed was truth. No dialogue could be built on falsehoods. These young Americans often fabricated imaginary backgrounds and names to cover their embarrassment.

Mrs. Joos had a plan to help these students. She would show them how to remodel their garments during long winter evenings. She would take a student into her shop where they would browse though fashion plates while making plans and working out small imperfections. When brought out in free, honest dialogue, the problems were easily corrected. For the most part the students who came to Mrs. Joos' sewing school were talented young ladies. Her main concern was having them accept themselves and their families for what they actually meant to this fast growing

In later years, these girls, having homes and families of their own, returned to thank Mrs. Joos for the guidance she had given them during their most critical years. These were the different years when they were so deeply embarrassed by the appearance of their foreign-born parents, their speech, manners, and even their names.

By 1910 tissue paper patterns were available through mail orders from New York at 12 cents each, postpaid, to subscribers to the Fashion Plate magazine.

Waiting time for the arrival of the patterns was reduced to three or four weeks which was considerably faster than today's pattern orders which take up to eight weeks to arrive.

From then on, dressmaking became easier and the task of teaching this craft became conceivably simpler. Although the early patterns were not what they are today, instructions were meager and difficult to understand by the inexperienced students.

Rural schools had improved so much that by 1912 only the best rated teachers were hired. This was an important step forward in elementary education. Some families were sendng their children after they reached age 12 to one of the academies which were being founded by the churches as private institutions.

Mrs. Joos found great delight in working with this new crop of students who were older and better qualified to read and understand instructions. Usually her students were of marriageable age. Therefore, it was of deep importance that they must have a course in sewing. Mothers advised their sons against marrying any young lady who could "not even sew her own clothes."

Ready-made clothes for women and children were still a few years away from appearing in shops and stores in the West Central Minnesota area. Every little village had several general merchandise stores which provided a healthy competition and stymied overcharging. All were stocked with bolts of fabric and sewing material along with spools of silk and cotton thread.

Mrs. Joos' dressmaking shop and sewing school worked at full capacity, six days a week, beginning in September with one week off for Christmas vacation. After the New Year, and until Easter, her students had no time off except for the weekends.

Soon after Easter, summer sewing began

with wedding finery, pretty dresses for the communicants and confirmands, which always included white shirts for boys. After July 4th, vacation began for Mrs. Joos and her business.

During the months of July and August the entire house was cleaned, painted, papered and varnished. Repairs were always needed in this busy household. Canning was done on a large scale with hundreds of jars of fruit, jams and jellies, and vegetables from the home garden. Wild fruit was plentiful in this area and the children expected to bring it home and they did so by the bucket full. All the village children enjoyed going to the farms of their families and friends where berries, cherries, gooseberries, currants and grapes grew in such abundance that they were welcome to pick all they could use. What wholesome summer fun this was

THE LAMP ON THE WINDOW SILL

And then came World War I which brought with it grief, concern, separations and heartbreaks to many families, including the Joos family. Although no family members had reached legal age, three left home to become involved in the war effort. None of them ever returned as permanent residents. Mrs. Joos' life style changed along with that of all Americans.

Styles in ladies' apparel went through the greatest change of any period in the history of our nation. Gone were the long sweeping skirts with their linings, multiple gores and exaggerated hem lines. Skirts moved up to shoe length, unlined and simple. This was considered so shocking that no lady of the older generation could accept the change. They continued to wear their long, lined skirts. Ivlilitary styles were the latest fashion, even to the color and weave of the fabrics.

Mrs. Joos was always first to accept the latest trend in fashions. She found all these changes refreshing and encouraged all her clients by pointing out the savings in yardage and sewing time.

Her sewing school suffered a lack of students as more and more young men were called into the service of our nation. Their sisters were required to take their places to assist in caring for the livestock and producing crops in greater abundance than ever before. Others became nurses or got involved in the war effort.

For the first time Mrs. Joos' school did not run its full ten month course. By mid summer it was evident that the Joos home would have too many vacant bedrooms through the winter.

Always a beehive of activity, the home was too quiet. In her simple way, she arranged to take in anyone who was in need of a room, with or without pay. She felt that this was her duty to help with the war effort.

By September she had two teachers from neighboring schools. A car load of students were encouraged to attend high school at St. Mary's Parochial School in Millerville by her offer of her home. All were happy to accept Mrs. Joos' hospitality and to pay for it.

Her sewing school had only day students that year. A pattern for the future was hereby set, and from then on she had only day students. All her boarders returned to their homes for weekends. This gave the Joos family time for togetherness, which was greatly needed during those tense months of having two sons overseas and those long intervals between letters.

"Idle hands are the devils workshop," is an old proverb that the Joos family often were reminded of by their father. While he kept his sons busy splitting and bringing in wood for the many stoves, Mrs. Joos kept her two daughters out of each other's hair by having them sort the many bags of snippings of wool, silk and velvet collected through her many years of sewing Nothing was ever wasted in her house. The scraps were pressed and placed into separate boxes. Mrs. Joos was amazed at the fine accumulation of usable material she had.

Our nation was at war. Families were short handed, while fine materials such as she had were no longer available. Therefore, Mrs. Joos felt that it must be put to good use because it all came from the materials her clients had brought and no longer had use for. Only in larger quantities, as she had now, would it make a worthwhile project. While it could be made into beautiful comfortable quilts, quantities of batting, linings and thread would be needed as well.

Not being a quilter herself, Mrs. Joos called upon her neighbor and dear friend, Mrs. Jake Thoennes, who was the champion quilter of the Millerville community. She knew all there was to know about making quilts, but she had no suggestion on how to acquire the funds to purchase the now costly linings, battings and thread for all those quilts. Costs had accelerated and were going up steadily. Together they decided that this was no project for two women. More quilters must be called into action. Via the old reliable "grape vine" method, a dozen ladies volunteered their services on a one evening a week basis.

At the first session it was decided that they would begin at once to sew two quilts. While this was going on each new volunteer agreed to sell tickets at 50 cents each or three for $1.00. All proceeds were to be used for worthy wartime causes. Mrs. Jake Thoennes was chosen as chair-man of this venture. Ticket books were made out of ruled tablet paper and distributed. It was decided that, each evening of the week, four members would come to Mrs. Joos' sewing room to work on the quilts until the two quilts were completed. After that new plans would be made.

The venture exceeded all their expectations. The quilts were indeed very beautiful and much admired as they were on display at A.J. Lorsung's store. The store had given the quilters special rates on all their purchases. All were happy. The quilters now had funds to purchase future needs for their project, while the two quilt winners also were very happy. All this activity was during a time in the lives of "those who stay home while their loved ones are away in foreign lands in great danger," namely the mothers.

The war ended with few casualties except for the aftermath which brought the longest, deepest depression the world has ever known and our nation endured. The escalated prices plunged almost overnight to a life threatening low.

Dress material for a pretty summer dress could be purchased for a nickel a yard with sewing thread thrown in free of charge, but everyone did not have the nickel to make the purchase.

Still Mrs. Joos' dressmaking shop was turning out well made comfortable garments. Most of them were made from recycled material obtained from the voluminous skirts and capes of earlier years. Day students continued to come chiefly to remake their own families' used clothing These were usually cut down to fit the smaller members.

All wool blankets were even cut and sewn into a coat so a child could attend school. Plush upholstery, which was ripped out of early abandoned automobiles and painstakingly washed, made warm coats and jackets for active little boys.

Mrs. Joos brought out her long neglected chart to design and cut patterns for this unusual type of fabric. As expected, the finished products were wonderfully warm and comfortable garments.

She spent her evenings, usually until midnight, using the lamp on the window sill to illuminate her machine. To the village it was a beacon of hope and well-being to all who passed by or cared to enter her comfortable home. Whether Mrs. Joos sewed or not, the kerosene lamp in the window always remained lit from dusk till dawn. Long after the home was electrified the kerosene lamp still burned in its accustomed place on the sill. When questioned about this, she smiled, but never gave anyone the reason for this.

By the end of the Thirties, the lean dry years slowly gave way. The economy was bedraggled from overuse, citizenry was undernourished, but still eager to believe that all this was passing away and a new more bountiful era was approaching.

At last, nature's life giving rains were falling again upon the parched fields, meadows, forests and paintless houses. Children of kindergarten age had never seen or experienced natural rainfall.

Soon after this, our mail boxes began to fill with colorful catalogs from mercantile business houses that no one had ever heard of before. They came in all sizes, from a few sheets hastily fastened with string and sent on their way to the bulky, heavy ones we know so well today. Whatever the size or weight, they were filled with colorful ready-to-wear women's garments and children's clothing. Everything was available at unheard of low prices, guaranteed to fit or your money would be returned cheerfully.

Rural Free Delivery (RFD) had its heyday as did all the overloaded wholesale houses. Rural mail carrier's vehicles were loaded with boxes of all sizes, bags, packages and even cream cans. Let us not forget the semiannual hat boxes filled with the latest creations in fine millinery.

While all this helped the economy of our cities, it was the death knell of all the many inland businesses which our founders had established. Most of these had been built into family shops such as Mrs. Joos' dressmaking and sewing school.

While Mrs. Joos had all the work she could do, it was the end of her sewing school. Why learn to sew when ready-mades were available at such low costs? Why indeed? City shops were also filling up with racks and more racks of women's and children's wearing apparel.

During the 35 years Mrs. Joos owned and managed her school and dressmaking shop she taught 264 young ladies of the Millerville community the artistic craft of sewing for themselves and their families. Uncounted are those who, through her unstinted friendship and help, became self reliant wives and helpmates to their husbands and mothers of their large families. It would be difficult to overestimate the benefits the contributed to this far-reaching area.

As the difficult years retire into oblivion, so the aging citizens willingly set aside tools and implements of their trade.

Time was also relieving Mrs. Joos of her busy life's work. Her husband Fredrick, no longer a young man, began to fail. Always in good health, he did not give in easily. After seven years of faithful nursing and care by his spouse and family, he passed away at home.

The life of ease and rest Mrs. Joos had deserved was now hers. The house, now so clean and quiet, was also cold and strange The children, except for one son, were all in homes of their own. She opened her beloved sewing machine which was still in its accustomed place in front of the window. The kerosene lamp was on its shelf No longer shiny from daily polishing she filled the sturdy bowl and gave it all a good rub down. As she was lovingly and leisurely polishing the old crystal chimney she suffered her first heart attack.

After many trips back and forth to the hospital, Mrs. Joos died a peaceful death on Thanksgiving Day in 1949.

Leaving behind so much yet undone, she had stacks of sewing material she intended to sew. She had plans to sew new draperies and curtains, rugs, cushions, new towels, sheets and pillow cases for her house as well as for gifts for her family and friends.

Frontier Home in Minnesota

Lumber Camp 1890's? Probably north of Park Rapids, location also known as Rails Prairie. Timber is second growth Norway pine.

Sod House—Lac qui Parle Co., ca. 1880

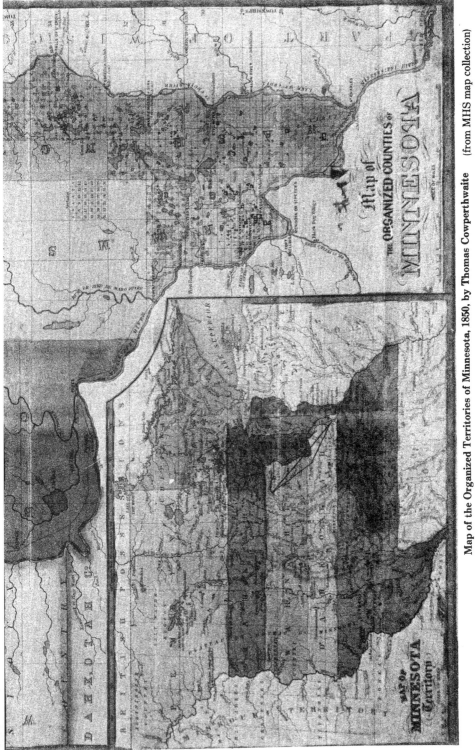

Map of the Organized Territories of Minnesota, 1850, by Thomas Cowperthwaite   (from MHS map collection)

Oxen Breaking Rolling Prairie

Pembina Dog Train—1856, ca 1859. Taken west 7th & Walnut Sts. Drivers: (left to right) Tarbell, Campbell

Pioneer Life near Rainy River

Order Form

Wagon Trails

Number of copies   _____

Name   _____

Street   _____

City, State   _____

ZIP Code   _____

Total copies @ $16.00 each $_____

Shipping and Handling @ $3.00 each $_____

Amount Enclosed $_____

Send orders to: Norma J. Van Amber Stanley, Distributor
                5804 Chastek Way
                Minnetonka MN 55345
                Phone: 952-934-3216
                e-mail: nstanley@wans.net

Or: VAN AMBER PUBLISHERS
                620 Elm Ave. E.
                Menomonie WI 54751
                Phone: 715-235-7702